IRAN

THE RISE OF THE REVOLUTIONARY GUARDS' FINANCIAL EMPIRE

How the Supreme Leader and the IRGC
Rob the People
to Fund International Terror

Iran: The Rise of the Revolutionary Guards' Financial Empire; How the Supreme Leader and the IRGC Rob the People to Fund International Terror

Copyright © National Council of Resistance of Iran – U.S. Representative Office, 2017.

First published in 2017 by
National Council of Resistance of Iran - U.S. Representative Office (NCRI-US),
1747 Pennsylvania Ave., NW, Suite 1125, Washington, DC 20006

ISBN-10: 1-944942-02-5
ISBN-13: 978-1-944942-02-1

Library of Congress Cataloging-in-Publication Data

National Council of Resistance of Iran - U.S. Representative Office.
Iran: The Rise of the Revolutionary Guards' Financial Empire; How the Supreme Leader and the IRGC Rob the People to Fund International Terror

1. Iran. 2. Economy. 3. Terrorism. 4. Corruption. 5. Revolutionary Guards

First Edition: March 2017

Printed in the United States of America

TABLE OF CONTENTS

THE NEW ECONOMIC STRUCTURE: A MIND-BOGGLING CONGLOMERATE OF 14 POWERHOUSES 73

DEALING WITH IRAN: INTERNAL KNOTS AND EXTERNAL OBSTACLES 123

EXECUTIVE SUMMARY

The Iran nuclear deal, finalized in July 2015 between the P5+1 world powers and Tehran, encouraged some in the West that the Iranian economy would finally turn a corner and be set on a path of gradual progress. Its implementation since January 2016, which brought the lifting of some international sanctions, strengthened these hopes, and Western companies initially expressed eagerness to ink deals with Tehran. But that optimism is increasingly being viewed as misplaced. Granted: marked improvements will take some time to materialize. Still, Iran's economy has not experienced the renaissance many anticipated.

International sanctions were never the cause of Iran's economic ills, which is why their lifting has not provided the cure. There are systemic, entrenched forces at play that have to do with the nature and sociopolitical roots of the political system in power today.

Iran's current chronic recession is primarily an outcome of a despotic regime's dogged attempts to survive despite a hostile domestic environment. Its rule is constantly challenged by a population largely excluded from legitimate political representation or material economic

Emblem of the IRGC, who, along with the Supreme Leader, have had a larger influence over the Iranian economy since 2005

benefits. This is the context that ought to be thoroughly examined in order to arrive at a realistic picture of Iran's economy.

Such an assessment begins with the peculiar configuration of capitalism in Iran over the past three decades. Economic development constantly coalescing with the pillars of political power, hides the origins of the current crisis, only heightened – not produced – by international sanctions.

This manuscript examines some vital factors and trends, including the overwhelming and accelerating influence (especially since 2005) of the Supreme Leader and the Islamic Revolutionary Guard Corps (IRGC). Credible evidence will be presented that runs counter to prevailing notions that the Iranian economy will undergo a rebirth simply through the lifting of sanctions. The reader is encouraged to scrutinize economic structure and players, as opposed to unsupported notions that sanctions relief will generate all-encompassing change regardless of the ruling system of *velayat-e faqih* (absolute clerical rule).

This study starts with property ownership, where an ever-increasing trend is revealed through which ownership of property in various spheres of the economy is gradually shifted from the population writ large towards a minority ruling elite comprised of the Supreme Leader's office and the IRGC.

Supreme Leader Ali Khamenei has been a driving force behind this silent seizure of Iran's private sector

This transformation is enabled by the regime's constitution, adopted in December 1979, all of the principles and articles of which regarding property ownership either deny or subvert respect for private property. Article 44 constitutionally splits the entire economy into three sectors: "state, cooperative, and private." The regime is granted legal justification to seize property by claiming adherence to "Islamic law," protection of "public interests," and "social justice." Article 49, for example, grants the regime "the responsibility of confiscating all wealth" that the state considers to be obtained through illegitimate means. As such, regime officials are unleashed in their large-scale and lucrative confiscation campaign.

Over the past decade, this has been billed as "privatization," and is the means by which a significant portion of Iran's economic institutions have been handed off to the office of the Supreme Leader and the security, military and economic apparatus under his auspices.

This so-called privatization campaign, which must be viewed as a decisive turning point, began in earnest in 2005, when Supreme Leader Ali Khamenei and the IRGC succeeded in closing ranks and stacking the executive with people who completely – at least initially – towed their line and shared Khamenei's strategic vision for the regime. At this point, Khamenei began to implement a profound restructuring of Iran's economy, in particular the ownership of a wide range of industries and institutions.

Over the ensuing eight years, the driving force behind all major economic developments would be the expansion of the sphere of influence of Khamenei's office and the IRGC over the country's economic resources, in order to intensify suppression, expand the reach of their adventurist policies, and advance the nuclear program. This was at the heart of the regime's attempts to ensure the continuation of its tenuous hold on power. Both the scale and pace of the expropriations – dubbed "privatization" – have been mind-boggling. The entire process was clearly rushed and chaotic, bringing with it the crippling and even destruction of many institutions.

Khamenei pursued three main policies: seizing state-owned firms and corporations; meddling in the financial markets; and eliminating public subsidies. This study offers a detailed account of how these policies were implemented, as well as their consequences, in order to provide a better understanding of the regime's current political and economic circumstances.

The first took the form of an official directive issued by Khamenei in May 2005. The government was instructed to transfer 80 percent of its economic enterprises to "non-government public, private and cooperative sectors" by the end of 2009. Among these were large mines, primary industries (including downstream oil and gas), foreign commerce, banks, insurance, power generation, post, roads, railroads, airlines, and shipping companies. By some estimates, close to $12B in shares were transferred over just three years, from 2005 to 2008. This compares to less than $1B from 1991 to 2004, a staggering 12-fold increase in one forth the time.

The beneficiaries of the bulk of these transfers were the Supreme Leader's office and its various tentacles, including the dominant *Setad*, the armed services, and the infamous *bonyads* or foundations. The implications of this stunning power-grab are better grasped in light of the fact that these institutions exercise virtually absolute control of all decision-making processes, legislative mechanisms, intelligence gathering and access to significant budgetary commitments. As a result, major powerhouses have arisen, which now act as the main players and consequently the gate keepers for western companies into the overall Iranian economy.

The consequent economic configuration is defined by at least 14 major economic powerhouses either directly or indirectly controlled by Khamenei, the IRGC or a combination of their affiliates. *Setad's* holdings alone, including real estate, corporate stakes and other assets, total about $95 billion, according to a recent Reuters calculation.

The second policy can perhaps most aptly be described as "devouring" the financial markets. When it comes to banks, financial and credit institutions, insurance, the stock market, domestic and foreign commerce, real-estate, and the financial instruments market, Khamenei's office has taken control over virtually everything that matters. This has been done through the so-called cooperatives (*ta'avoni*), some of the most important of which are among the 14 economic blocks.

In July 2006, Khamenei issued another order clarifying "the general policies of developing various nongovernmental sectors," and organizing the country's economy around the IRGC and *Bassij* cooperatives, and the foundations controlled by the Supreme Leader, especially *Setad*. Notably, the directive identifies the purposes for which the resultant revenues should be used, including committing 30 percent to the cooperatives, and providing incentives to strengthen them.

Then, in 2008, "banking system reforms" transformed the country's banks into conduits for simple and cheap cash grabs by enterprises controlled by the Supreme Leader. A large number of financial and credit institutions were created. Next, some of them were made into private banks. 31 Iranian banks and a number of financial, commercial and industrial enterprises belonging to each of the cooperatives have been identified in this book. Still, officials of the Iranian regime have estimated that the number of large firms owned by these banks ranges anywhere from 600 to over 1,000.

A small number of IRGC affiliates and Khamenei aides — who primarily ran foundations' economic activities as well as companies owned by Khamenei's office and the armed forces — gained easy access to low-interest loans. According to the central bank, 29 percent of bank deposits have been loaned to just 173 applicants in the entire country. Each of these applicants received loans valued at over $16 million. The majority of these loans have never been paid back to the banks, resulting in a financial crisis in its own right.

Perhaps the most glaring example of the corruption in Iran is the easy access that IRGC members have to loan interest loans. 29% of the country's bank deposits have been loaned to just 173 applicants, with each of these applicants receiving a loan worth at least $16 million.

The third policy, cutting subsidies, took effect in 2010, and marked arguably the biggest economic transformation in Iran since the land reforms of 1962. When the price of gasoline increased 21-fold and the price of natural gas increased seven-fold, manufacturing costs sky-rocketed. A large portion of production facilities, an estimated 60-70 percent, were either shut down or had their capacity reduced to less than a third. Their market share is now dominated by the *velayat-e faqih's* commercial enterprises which, after raising the required capital, are now flooding the market with imported products.

The elimination of subsidies has, in effect, accelerated the monopolization of financial markets and broad-based economic activity. It has brought about the annihilation of a large segment of the manufacturing sector and hurtled the inflation rate out of control.

These three policies, namely seizure of public property creating economic powerhouses, near-absolute control over financial markets, and elimination of subsidies, are all means to a single end: the wholesale and sweeping confiscation of public wealth and assets for the benefit of Khamenei and the IRGC. But where do the astronomical profits go?

In later chapters, the book traces how the money ends up funding the conflict in Syria, terrorism and sectarianism in Iraq, the war in Yemen, the nuclear and missile programs, the security apparatus in Iran, and fundamentalist operations around the world. In the end, Iran's national economy has been made to serve, in large part, the domestic suppression, warmongering, export of fundamentalism, and terrorism.

A year after the JCPOA brought about the lifting of sanctions, foreign companies are exhibiting profound caution – contrary to earlier expectations and voices of optimism – about dealing with Iran or investing in the country. Domestically, since the *velayat-e faqih* and its affiliates have taken hold of a vast portion of the Iranian economy, particularly banking and financial institutions as well as profitable factories and trade organizations, in practice all foreign deals will be made with them. Foreign investors cannot in practical terms avoid entanglement by affiliation in the Iranian regime's behavior, including its support for terrorism, continued aggressive policies towards regional countries, manufacture and testing of ballistic missiles, and systematic egregious human rights violations inside Iran.

With good reason, western banks and companies continue to harbor mistrust and doubt, and remain cautious about the high risk of doing business in Iran. In reality, the back-breaking control of the regime over the entire economic system and the astonishing growth of extremely disruptive and obstructive rules and regulations severely limit freedom of action, leaving little or no room for genuine free-market competition in Iran. Analysts estimate that two thirds of Iran's total industrial capacity has either vanished or remains idle.

The plethora of threats and restrictions facing foreign investors include international bans or penalties for certain transactions, concerns about new sanctions being implemented through the "snapback" mechanisms envisioned in the nuclear deal, and U.S. congressional opposition to doing business with Iran in general.

Moreover, there are fundamental domestic issues at play, stemming in essence from the gridlock brought about by the policies of the Iranian regime. The economy is suffering from profound financial instability, the most visible manifestations of which are bankruptcies in the collapsing banking sector. Spontaneous decision-making has sowed confusion and instability in banking rules and policy, creating extreme difficulties relevant to regulation for foreign investments and even registering a company. A plethora of onerous rules and regulations muddy the waters.

Other domestic hurdles include the current recession in Iran; pervasive corruption, aspects of which are subject to violations of U.S. and European laws; lack of genuine competition; inadequate infrastructure for communications and transportation; and no guarantees or secure laws and regulations.

The ruling regime, and by extension the economy, are further destabilized by political infighting at the pinnacle of the regime's hierarchy, aggravated by the probability of Khamenei's death in the near term and ensuing conflict to determine his replacement.

Western companies engaged in economic and financial deals with Iran would like to portray their activities as transactions with the "private sector." However, behind the official banks and companies lies a web of institutions controlled by the theocracy, and specifically the IRGC. Western companies, governments and the citizens they represent cannot avoid the reality that today the gate keepers to Iran's economy are those who suppress the Iranian population and export the very terrorism and fundamentalist ideology that threaten the West.

There are important conclusions here. First, the vast and interconnected network of wealth and power in the hands of the *velayat-e faqih* is indicative of a sophisticated monopoly over the Iranian economy. Put simply, to do business with Iran is to do business with Khamenei and the IRGC.

Second, the disastrous economic situation – unemployment, inflation, near-destruction of the manufacturing sector, wide-scale corruption, stagnant wages, etc. – is the most enduring long-term source for social discontent. It is a major source of instability for the regime at home, casting a long shadow of uncertainty over its future.

The growing monopolization of the Iranian economy has translated into circumstances that create enormous hurdles to true economic growth and development in Iran. Sanctions relief will not change these deeply entrenched factors. As social demands grow in breadth and depth, the regime's ability to respond to them becomes increasingly limited. That presents a recipe for a major social transformation, one that sees no future role for Tehran's theocratic rulers.

INTRODUCTION

The events unfolding since the signing of the nuclear agreement – the Joint Comprehensive Plan of Action or JCPOA – between Iran and six global powers, coupled with the lifting of sanctions and an uptick in oil exports by Iran back to pre-sanctions levels, have failed to pull the Iranian economy out of a seemingly never-ending recession. An essentially structural and systemic misfortune has plagued Iran's economic and political life, something that cannot be scrutinized within the narrow confines of sanctions effects. This underscores the need for a careful analysis of the profound and interconnected roots of Iran's problems.

Posing are representatives of Iran and the six global powers that signed the JCPOA, an ineffective agreement that failed to bolster Iran's economy

Recession in Iran deepened despite the lifting of sanctions following the nuke deal

A wide-ranging and serious examination is in order, one that uncovers the mechanisms and dynamics that define Iran's current regime and motivate its strategic tendencies. It must trace Tehran's ideology, political attributes, and the imperatives it faces for the preservation of its rule as it tries to keep at bay an overwhelmingly disenfranchised and disaffected citizenry. Such an examination would ultimately reveal if the current chronic recession is a product of political imperatives for the regime's survival, or a function of other factors. More specifically, does the peculiar configuration of capitalist development in Iran over the past three decades, constantly coalescing with the pillars of political power, bear any relation to the origins of the current economic crisis?

Prior to examining such questions, let us first ask: Can the "privatization" of a significant portion of Iran's economic institutions – which have largely been handed off to the office of the Supreme Leader and the security, military and economic apparatus under his auspices – be viewed as a decisive and seminal development, or should it be perceived as relatively trivial or uninteresting?

In order to scrutinize Iran's political economy in the past four decades, we shall focus our attention on the status of property ownership, which appears to be a salient feature of the events unfolding during the period under study. An ever-increasing trend is revealed in which ownership of property in multiple spheres of economic livelihood is gradually taken from the Iranian people at large and shifted into the hands of the minority ruling elite.

THE "CONSTITUTIONAL" BACKDROP

ran's current political system is a theocracy (or religious dictatorship) founded on the principle of *velayat-e faqih* or absolute clerical rule through a Supreme Leader. In its constitution, adopted in December 1979, all principles and articles that mention property ownership are, without exception, tethered to restrictions and limitations that either deny or subvert respect for private property.

Article 40 of the Constitution states, "No one is entitled to exercise his rights in a way injurious to others or detrimental to public interests."[1]

Article 44 splits the economy into the three sectors of "state, cooperative, and private," adding: "Ownership in each of these three sectors is protected by the laws of the Islamic Republic, in so far as this ownership is in conformity with the other articles of this chapter, does not go beyond the bounds of Islamic law, contributes to the economic growth and progress of the country and does not harm society."[2]

Hence, legal support for ownership or proprietorship has four provisos, some of which are difficult if not impossible to fulfill: first, conformity with all the other articles of Chapter Four, Economy

Iranian regime operates as a theocracy

---

[1]   Constitution of the Islamic Republic of Iran, Official Website of the Islamic Republic of Iran Permanent Mission to the United States, www.iran-un.org/en/constitution, Article 40.

[2]   Ibid., Article 44, section 5.

and Financial Affairs; second, conformity with "Islamic law;" third, enhancement of the economic progress of the country; and, fourth, avoiding harm to society.

Article 47 states that private ownership is restricted to property obtained through "legitimate" means, the criteria for which are defined "by law": "Private ownership, legitimately acquired, is to be respected. The relevant criteria are determined by law."[3]

The qualifications stipulated in these clauses are justified with references to such objectives as protecting the "public interest," "social justice" or "Islamic law." But, in reality, the practice of seizing private or public property by the regime has turned into a lucrative venture for the ruling elite, one that undermines and causes significant harm to social development and public interests. The constitution of the *velayat-e faqih* provides a legal and lawful basis for denying the principle of ownership, with each of the articles in Chapter IV enabling the regime to systematically and brazenly snatch private property in various economic spheres:

- ☑ Article 31 is misused for confiscation of land;

- ☑ Article 44 facilitates the effortless seizure of public institutions at discounted rates by bodies and forces tied to the Supreme Leader's office;

- ☑ Article 147 is cited in legislation, specifically enabling the Islamic Revolutionary Guard Corps (IRGC) and its affiliate Bassij to extend their domination over the economy;[1]

- ☑ And, articles 45 and 49 are relied upon for the seizure of public and private assets and properties by the Supreme Leader.

In Article 49, "The government has the responsibility of confiscating all wealth accumulated through usury, usurpation, bribery, embezzlement, theft, gambling, misuse of endowments, misuse of government contracts and transactions, the sale of uncultivated lands and other resources subject to public ownership, the operation of centers of corruption, and other illicit means and sources, and restoring it to its legitimate owner; and if no such owner can be identified, it must be entrusted to the public treasury."[4]

---

[3] Ibid., Article 47.

[4] Constitution of the Islamic Republic of Iran, Official Website of the Islamic Republic of Iran Permanent Mission to the United States, www.iran-un.org/en/constitution, Article 49.

The Iranian regime's Constitution explicitly allows the confiscation of land, property, wealth and companies

The regime's first Supreme Leader, Ruhollah Khomeini, and his successor, Ali Khamenei, turned this article into a strategic law through which not only assets with unidentified owners but also other people's assets, residences, money and inheritance, in addition to public property, land, forests and public companies were seized through dubious schemes, intimidation or the use of force. Tens of thousands of political opponents have been victimized by such seizures merely for displaying sentiments deemed challenging to the regime.

The third clause of the executive law for Article 49 states: "In order to implement Article 49, the High Judicial Council shall form a branch or branches of the Revolutionary Court in the capital of each of the provinces or cities, as it sees fit, to review and establish Sharia requirements with respect to all claims." In other words, the court is established not to review legal claims made by those whose property has been seized, but to "establish Sharia requirements" for the seizures themselves.

THE MAJLIS (PARLIAMENT) PROVIDES LEGISLATIVE LICENSE

In accordance with the predominant spirit of the constitution regarding property seizures, both the "Revolutionary Council" in 1979 and the "Islamic Consultative Assembly" (parliament or *Majlis*) in the ensuing years have passed numerous resolutions and regulations enabling the mullahs and their cronies to unilaterally confiscate property in various spheres.

In the 1980s, the seizure of public lands began in earnest, and the rate of confiscations quickly accelerated. In the 1990s, the "air rights" (space above land) in cities, previously thought to belong to the public domain, were seized and municipalities for which the central government was reluctant to allocate funding in the annual budget instead found new sources of revenue by literally "selling density." Thereafter, a range of other interests were seized or confiscated, among them public gardens and green spaces in cities, farmlands, villages in the outskirts of cities, and even beaches and

The Majlis (Parliament) Provides Legislative License for Confiscation of Wealth

forests situated in the northern province of Mazandaran (Caspian Sea), to name a few.

The Property Rights Alliance's 2016 International Property Rights Index (IPRI) ranks 128 countries, representing 98 percent of world Gross Domestic Product and 93 percent of the world's population, comparing the protection of property rights – physical and intellectual – across countries. The index ranks Iran at 101 (out of 128).[5]

These trends have continued unabated since 1979, but they accelerated in the 2000s with the domination of the *velayat-e faqih* (Supreme Leader) over the bulk of the Iranian economy.

Iran ranks near the worst in the world in terms of property rights

---

[5] International Property Rights Index 2016 Report;
http://internationalpropertyrightsindex.org/countries

AN ECONOMIC
BEHEMOTH
WREAKING HAVOC

Today, Iran's economic ills comprise a bafflingly long list: from anemic economic growth to the swelling ranks of the unemployed; from a preposterous bulge in the money supply and the almost bankrupt banking sector to the rapid environmental ruin. An overview of mismanagement on so vast a scale, and what can only be described as structural devastation, reveals that the determining factor – out of which other challenges arise directly or indirectly – remains to be the domination and control of Khamenei's empire and its military arm, the IRGC, over the country's economy. Judging by its modus operandi, especially over the last decade, this element has proved to have an extremely pernicious influence.

Some economists and analysts prescribe a way out of the current crisis through "restraining inflation and inflationary forces" or "turning away from an economic model based on mercantilism, usury and corruption towards a manufacturing-based economy." Restraining inflation, shifting towards manufacturing, boosting capital growth, shunning mercantilism, and other similar policies can be productive in and of themselves. They can certainly lead to improvements in the absence of structural barriers. But, there are enormous structural obstacles in Iran. Simply falling back on these

Iran is struggling with a rising unemployment rate

recommendations would wittingly or unwittingly have us close our eyes to the most fundamental hurdles.

Multiple layers of corruption coating the entire edifice of the economy, together with the intense rivalry among the regime's unrestrained factions seeking to grab a larger share of the pie, provide the main avenues for the large-scale transfer of social wealth to a ruling minority. But the sheer gravity of the catastrophe cannot be downgraded to these elements alone, though they produce chronic challenges. If, instead of zooming in on each of the components of the current crisis, we step back and consider the root cause of the problem, we invariably arrive at the "absolute" clerical rule (*velayat-e faqih*) and its core policies. The ruling theocracy has made the Iranian economy subservient to its own survival.

One cannot accurately analyze the chaos, famine and extraordinary inflation of the early 1940s in Iran without studying the role of the military occupation of Iran by the Allies, which acted as a prelude to the wholesale plunder of the country's wealth. Similarly, the downward economic spiral of the 1980s cannot be properly grasped

The Iran Iraq War helped precipitate Iran's economic downturn

without considering the decisive influence of the eight-year Iran-Iraq war. And today, a serious study of the economic malaise gripping Iran cannot be beneficial without considering the root causes of the problem, and especially the economy's vast transformation in recent years, as the office of the Supreme Leader has aggressively pursued its interests at the domestic, regional and international levels.

This study shines the spotlight on these root causes by attempting to map out the trajectory and consequences of Iran's political economy over the past decade.

"THE CAT ATE MAZANDARAN"

During his reign beginning in the early 1920s, Iran's Reza Shah (king) became the largest land owner almost overnight. Today, that title belongs to the Iranian regime's Supreme Leader Ali Khamenei and his vast financial empire.

Mazandaran Province near The Caspian Sea

The title of this chapter (The Cat Ate Mazandaran) is borrowed from a political cartoon published in the French daily *L'Humanité* on March 4, 1937. It depicted Reza Shah Pahlavi as a Persian cat taking a big bite out of Iran's entire northern province of Mazandaran.[6] It poked fun at one of Reza Shah's infamous tactics: using fear and force to confiscate and grab vast tracts of land from landowners and farmers alike. In this way, he became the owner of numerous villages and large swathes of fertile land. By the end of his rule in 1941, it is estimated that Reza Shah owned 2,670 entire villages, an extraordinary feat for a man who owned not a single parcel of land before coming to power.[7]

In the context of this general tendency by tyrannies that have ruled Iran, we should pay particular attention to the peculiar features of the current *velayat-e faqih* system. These attributes are a function of its medieval nature and inherent weaknesses in coping

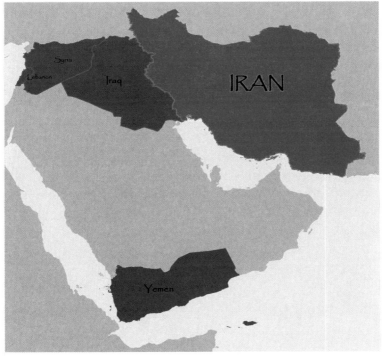

Iranian officials believe they have "extended its (Iran's) dominion over four Arab capitals," in Beirut, Damascus, Baghdad, and Sana'a.

---

[6]   Mahmoud Pourshalchi, *Cossak*, based on documents archived by the French Foreign Ministry

[7]   Mohammad Amjad, *A History of Iran's Political Economy.*

with the demands of the modern world. In addition to its inexorable need to suppress the rest of society as a whole, the regime's nature also dictates export of terrorism and fundamentalism, developing nuclear weapons and closing ranks, i.e. consolidating the exclusive authority of the *velayat-e faqih* over all aspects of Iranian society.

One of the most complex tasks vis-à-vis the regime is to understand and arrive at the real spirit behind each of these policies. For example, is the regime's adventurism in the region and boasts of "extending its dominion over four Arab capitals" indicative of its true strength, or of strategic weaknesses that need to be hidden behind an empty show of tactical power?

The mullahs' unambiguous political and military meddling in regional countries, coupled with the propaganda and psychological warfare, not to mention the hyperbole and the undeserved praise showered on Tehran by those in the West seeking to accommodate and appease it, fall far short of painting a "powerful" Iran. Such misguided affirmations are ill-suited to an appreciation of the facts: the main motivator behind the regime's behavior in the region is its inescapable need to ward off existential crises and threats brewing in society and even inside the regime's own corridors of power.

In other words, such posturing by Tehran is key to its survival while it nevertheless lays bare its structural weaknesses and vulnerabilities to the trained eye. If these policies signaled strength, then logically they would be backed by formidable and genuine foundations (for example, by a serious popular mandate). Absent such foundations, when such posturing reaches its apex, the regime's strategy begins to unravel.

CLOSING RANKS

The same logic applies to the regime's attempts to close ranks, cementing the exclusive authority of the *velayat-e faqih*, its efforts to dominate the region, and its prevailing control over all aspects of the Iranian economy.

No other period tells us more about the course of contraction and tightening of the regime's ranks than the eight-year tenure of Tehran's firebrand president Mahmoud Ahmadinejad (2005-2013). During this period, when compared not just to its own three-and-a-half-decade history but also to that of the broader history of Iran since Nader Shah (1747), the ruling regime was at the height of its power. It had an influential regional stature, the dominant faction had succeeded in marginalizing rivals, serious suppressive measures had been intensified against the organized opposition, and Tehran's coffers were brimming with cash from oil exports.

In the early 2000s, the United States, the world's sole superpower, found itself in a position in the Middle East that invariably benefited the Iranian regime. Both the eastern and western rivals of Tehran were ousted (in Iraq and Afghanistan). As Tehran cast its menacing shadow over Iraq in the aftermath of the 2003 invasion, it discovered additional avenues to meddle in the affairs of other regional countries. Meanwhile, the main Iranian opposition the Mujahedin-e Khalq (MEK) had voluntarily disarmed in 2003 in Camp Ashraf, Iraq.[8] Energized by a trillion dollars in his foreign currency reserves, Khamenei seized an exceptional and unprecedented opportunity to advance his goals. He engineered the regime's presidential elections to bring to power a subservient government. He also united the disparate elements of his faction under the rubric of "fundamentalists," thus extending his control over the Majlis. He also eliminated subsidies, heralding the largest

---

[8] After discussions with the Multi-National Force, Iraq, the MEK handed over its weapons, including "2,139 tanks, armored personnel carriers, artillery pieces, air defense artillery pieces and miscellaneous vehicles," as well as thousands of light weapons and ammunition. See: (http://www.armed-services.senate.gov/imo/media/doc/4-CENTCOM,%20MAY%2017,%202003.pdf) In return, the United States made a commitment to protect its members as 'protected persons' under the Fourth Geneva Convention.

IRAN: THE RISE OF THE REVOLUTIONARY GUARDS' FINANCIAL EMPIRE

economic transformation in Iranian history, which neither the Shah (prior to 1979) nor the regime's previous presidents like Ali Akbar Hashemi Rafsanjani or Mohammad Khatami had dared to implement. He then expropriated many industrial, financial, commercial, real-estate and agricultural ventures, allowing him to cast an extensive shadow over most of the country's economy.

PROFOUND RESTRUCTURING OF IRAN'S ECONOMY

THE YEAR 2005, A WATERSHED MOMENT

I n the history of Iran's political economy, the year 2005 marks a watershed moment. It was at that juncture that Khamenei embarked on a profound restructuring of Iran's economy, especially when it comes to the ownership of a wide range of industries and institutions. Over the ensuing eight years, the driving force behind all major economic developments would be the expansion of the sphere of influence of Khamenei's office and the IRGC over the country's economic resources, in order to intensify suppression, expand the reach of their adventurist policies, and, it goes without saying, advance the nuclear program. This was at the heart of the regime's attempts to ensure the continuation of its tenuous hold on power.

The events of this period were tantamount to stripping the Iranian people of their public property and ferociously depleting their financial reserves. This theme has, of course, been characteristic of all the regime's various phases. Its routine methods have always included applying various types of extortion, imposing unjust taxes, hiking consumer prices, suppressing incomes for workers and laborers, delaying the payment of wages, flooding the market with low-quality products sold at unjustifiably elevated prices, and resorting to brutal force and violence to reach its objectives. Yet the events that unfolded after 2005 were unique in that they happened in the main with Khamenei's personal intervention.

- ☑ Firstly, the methods and processes of implementation were extraordinary in their own right;
- ☑ Secondly, the scale of expropriations was unprecedented, leading to the rise of major monopolies;
- ☑ And thirdly, the process was tangibly rushed and chaotic, bringing with it the destruction or at least crippling of many institutions, not to mention the shredding of rules and regulations governing the bureaucratic, financial and monetary systems.

The three major policies pursued by Khamenei were the expropriation of government-owned firms and corporations;

interference in the financial markets; and elimination of public subsidies. A detailed account of how these policies were implemented as well as their consequences will provide a better understanding of the regime's current political and economic circumstances.

EXPROPRIATION OF STATE-OWNED ENTERPRISES

Although the so-called privatization policy justified under Article 44 of the Constitution began in the 1990s and continued into the presidencies of Ali Akbar Hashemi Rafsanjani (1989-1997) and Mohammad Khatami (1997-2005), it nonetheless moved at a sluggish pace. It was Khamenei's personal directive in 2005, which transformed this policy both in terms of style of execution as well as substance.

In the Directives on the General Policies Concerning Article 44, issued by Khamenei on May 22, 2005,[9] the government was instructed to transfer 80 percent of its economic enterprises to "non-government public, private and cooperative sectors" by the end of the Fourth Plan (2009). These included: large mines, primary industries (including downstream oil and gas), foreign commerce, banks, insurance, power generation, post, roads, railroads, airlines, and shipping companies.

Several official reports and records confirm that Khamenei's decision in 2005 marked a leap for the *velayat-e faqih's* command over the Iranian economy. A report published by the regime's Ministry of Economic Affairs and Finance states, "The overall policies of Article 44 ... form the basis of the country's economy, ... a charter for running the country's economic affairs ... and

---

[9] "Text of the Directive of the Supreme Leader Regarding the General Policies of Article 44," Expediency Council website, May 22, 2005. (In Farsi). <www.maslehat. ir/Contents.aspx? p=c4eaa3d8-2de0-45c5-8ad9-9004a79af493>

The IRGC and the Ayatollahs seize private property and industry

the most important priority for the overall management of the country's economy."[10] An October 2009 report by the parliament's research center refers to Khamenei's decision, stating: "... In 2005, privatization in Iran entered a new phase, which bears fundamental distinctions with previous initiatives when it comes to the nature and scope of execution. Per the mandated policies, the government has been instructed to transfer the ownership of all its economic activities to accelerate national economic growth." Referring to a review of the mechanisms of transferring the ownership of 264 companies between the years 2005 and 2009, the report concludes: "The Iranian economy is going through a phase that will see its transformation from a state-run economy to a semi state-run economy instead of going from a state-run to a privatized economy."

However, the oft-cited "semi state-run" phrase or what official documents refer to as the "non-government public sector" is in reality a pseudonym for the extensive sector that is now controlled by the Supreme Leader's office and its affiliates. For a picture of this tremendous transformation in Iran's economy, we can refer

---

[10] Ministry of Economic Affairs and Finance, Second Report on the Progress of the Implementation of the General Policies of Article 44, September 2009.

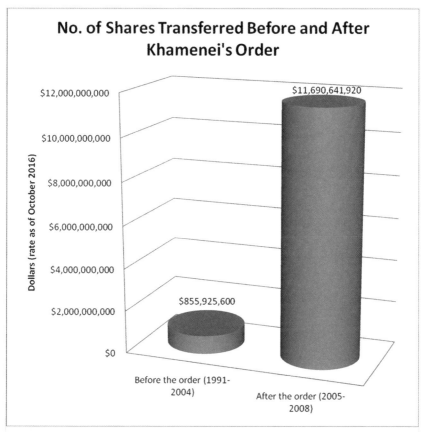

Source: Ministry of Economic Affairs and Finance, first report on the implementation of the Fourth Program Law

to the Ministry of Economic Affairs and Finance report,[11] which presents a graph that compares the transfer of ownership before and after Khamenei's directive.

This report also provides another graph showing that the transferred ownership during the first term of Ahmadinejad's presidency accounted for up to 93 percent of the total amount transferred.

This new economic landscape, the composition of which has marked the most significant political and economic makeover of the last decade, has taken shape on the foundation of the unlimited and

---

[11] Ministry of Economic Affairs and Finance, Report on the Implementation of the law to reform provisions of the Fourth Economic, Social and Cultural Development Program of the Islamic Republic of Iran, and implementation of the general policies of Article 44 of the Constitution.

unchallenged expansion of the so-called "public sector." The role of the main employer of the country has been switched from the government to the *velayat-e faqih*.

A study conducted in 2012 shows that "the application of the privatization policy in relation to the 'relinquishment of enterprises under the title of transfer of ownership to the private sector' over the 11 years ending in 2011 happened in a way that the public non-government sector has the largest share of these enterprises at 35.78 percent. The government sector, at 25.27 percent, is second, the cooperatives and justice shares have a total of 21.11 percent at third place and the private sector follows it with 4.91 percent."[12]

Although according to the above-mentioned study, the *velayat-e faqih* and its various arms (*Setad- Ejraiy-e Farman-e Hazrat-e Emam* or Headquarters for Executing the Order of the Imam; the armed services; and the *bonyad*s or foundations) have taken ownership of close to 36 percent of commercial enterprises, in practice they exercise a quantitative and qualitative economic hegemony because of their virtually absolute control over all decision-making processes, legislative mechanisms, intelligence-gathering, and access to a significant portion of the annual budget.

---

[12]   Akhoundi and Co. Research, Tejarat Weekly, March 13, 2015

THE 14 POWERHOUSES

The above statistics from 2012 do not paint a sufficiently comprehensive picture of the process that saw the transformation of ownership and management of economic enterprises and their complete relinquishment to the *velayat-e faqih*, firstly because this process continued after their publication through 2015.[13]

Secondly, the confiscation of some assets, especially through Khamenei's *Setad* takes place through the use of force and is not mentioned in the official accounts of so-called privatization. A 2013 Reuters investigation lists some examples of *Setad's* unjust confiscation of houses, assets, and properties due to "vacancies" or due to their ownership by religious minorities like the Bahais.[14]

Nevertheless, the insatiable appetite of Khamenei's office for more assets has reached new heights. According to

The Setad unjustly confiscate property, often targeting religious minorities such as the Bahais. Pictured above is a Bahai shrine in the Iranian city of Babol, which was destroyed in April 2004.

---

[13] Jafar Sobhani, advisor to the president of the Privatization Organization: "This year, the transfer of companies will end. ... There are 200 companies remaining. According to plans, these companies will be transferred by the end of the year." Kasb-o-Kar website, April 8, 2015.

[14] "Assets of the Ayatollah, Reuters, November 11, 2013.

media reports, *Setad* has also confiscated everything from heritage properties to the "Farahabad polo and horse riding club." According to a research study, "Out of roughly 10,000 reviewed cases in the *Setad* over the past 17 years ... about 50 percent of the cases were related to Muslim Iranians who have traveled abroad, and who have had all or a portion of their belongings confiscated merely because they resided outside the country."[15]

Thirdly, beyond what they have gained from the transfers under Article 44, the new economic blocks and especially *Setad*

Ali Ashraf Afkhami implemented the seizure of diverse sections of industry

have adopted an aggressive strategy to obtain ownership of other sectors. The chair of the board of the *"Tadbir* Economic Development Group," Ali Ashraf Afkhami, has said: "Gradually, we defined the strategy of our presence in various fields. With this goal in mind, a strong team of experts formulated a strategic plan for us to enter a range of investment areas."[16]

A comparative analysis of all such events confirms that the rate of confiscation over the past decade, which has reshaped the Iranian economy, has accelerated at an unprecedented rate. All the data point to one factor at the heart of the political, economic events of this period: an unrivaled role played by Khamenei's office in influencing and setting the trend. Moreover, that office has transferred the most profitable and the largest enterprises to its own venture, *Setad*.

An exhaustive list of all the foundations and their affiliates is unmanageable. For an overview of the new composition of economic enterprises and blocks that have taken shape or evolved over the past decade, suffice it to say that the new economic

---

[15] Baztab website, November 23, 2013

[16] Sharq daily, April 16, 2013

establishment, outside of the government-owned companies, can be generally seen in the context of the 14 powerhouses listed below:

1. The Headquarters for Executing the Order of the Imam (*Setad*)

2. The *Mostazafan* (Oppressed) Foundation

3. *Astan-e Qods-e Razavi*

4. *Shahid* (Martyr) Foundation

5. *Emdad* (Aid) Committee

6. The Islamic Revolutionary Guard Corps (IRGC) Cooperative Foundation

7. The *Khatam al-Anbiya* Construction Headquarters

8. The Cooperative Foundation of the *Bassij* Force

9. The *Ghadir* Investment Company

10. The Armed Forces Social Welfare Investment Organization (SATA)

11. *Khatam al-Osia* Construction Headquarters

12. The Cooperative Foundation of the State Security Forces (NAJA)

13. The Cooperative Foundation of the Army (BTAJA)

14. The Cooperative Foundation of the Armed Forces Joint Chiefs of Staff (VDJA)

DEVOURING THE FINANCIAL MARKETS

The list of companies, investment holdings, land parcels, real estate, and all sorts of other categories of assets that have been poured into the coffers of Khamenei's office and the IRGC is truly mindboggling. These institutions have been the primary means of making astronomical sums of money in the financial markets. Mercantilism is essentially unruly, but the *velayat-e faqih* model of mercantilism, rooted in its penchant for monopolies, is doubly belligerent. When it comes to the non-manufacturing sector (banks, financial and credit institutions, insurance, the stock market and beyond, domestic and foreign commerce, real-estate, and the financial products market), Khamenei's office has devoured virtually everything that matters. This has been done through the so-called cooperatives, some of the most important of which are among the 14 economic blocks.

Although some of these cooperatives were founded years ago, since 2005 their entry into the financial markets has taken an aggressive turn, conjuring up images of the ruthless military assaults of the Mongols. Khamenei himself in his March 2005 directive opened the floodgates for the tidal wave of cooperatives and their entry into these markets. In his order, Khamenei asserts that the cooperatives' share in the economy must reach 25 percent by 2014 (the end of the Fifth Program). Additionally, the government must support these cooperatives through tax and credit incentives involving "all the country's financial institutions." It must also "remove all barriers and constraints" on the entry of cooperatives into all spheres, including banking and insurance, and provide support "to enable cooperatives to gain market access."[2]

A year later, on July 3, 2006, Khamenei issued another order clarifying "the general policies of developing various nongovernmental sectors," and organizing the country's economy around the IRGC and *Bassij* cooperatives and foundations controlled by the Supreme Leader, especially *Setad*. Notably, the directive identifies the purposes for which the revenues of such transfers should be used, including:

- ☑ Committing 30 percent of the transfer revenues to the cooperatives
- ☑ Providing incentives to strengthen the cooperatives

The practical meaning of these orders is simply that Khamenei in 2005 monopolized financial markets (banks, insurance, the stock market, etc.). A year later, he re-routed the revenues that the government obtained from the sale of assets towards the IRGC and *Bassij* cooperatives.

In 2015, first Abbas Akhundi, the Minister of Roads and Urban Development, and later Eshaq Jahangiri, First Deputy to the regime's president, questioned where the more than $100B in revenues obtained from the sale of government-owned assets had gone.[3]

A decade earlier, Khamenei had explicitly ordered that these revenues go to the Supreme Leader's coffers. The decisions adopted in 2008 in the context of the "banking system reforms" transformed the country's banks into conduits for simple and cheap cash grabs for enterprises controlled by the Supreme Leader.

	2010	2011	2012	2013
LOANS TO "NON-GOVERN-MENT" SECTOR	$91,408,000,000	$108,744,000,000	$127,971,200,000	$151,926,400,000

Source: Iran's Central Bank

The *velayat-e faqih's* actions with respect to Iran's financial markets can be summarized as follows:

Firstly, regarding cooperatives, a large number of financial and credit institutions were created. Next, some of them were made into private banks. In 1979, there were 36 banks and funds. By 2014, according to official reports, the number of these institutions had ballooned to 31 state-owned and private banks, 36 legal leasing agencies, over 460 illegal leasing agencies, close to 1,000 legal credit unions, and 7,000 illegal financial and credit institutions.[4]

The table below lists 31 Iranian banks and the number of financial, commercial and industrial enterprises belonging to each, based on reports published by Iranian media outlets. The total number of institutions in this table is 309, but, officials of the Iranian regime have put the number of such bank-owned firms anywhere from 600 to over 1,000.[17]

	BANK NAME	AFFILIATION	NO. OF COMPANIES OWNED BY BANK	NO. OF BRANCHES
1	KESHAVARZI (AGRICULTURE)	GOVERNMENT	7	1928
2	SEPAH	GOVERNMENT	4	1754
3	POST BANK	GOVERNMENT	1	406
4	MELLI (NATIONAL)	GOVERNMENT	26	3325
5	EXPORTS DEVELOPMENT OF IRAN (TOSE'E SADERAT-E IRAN)	GOVERNMENT	5	40
6	INDUSTRY AND MINING (SAN'AT VA MA'DAN)	GOVERNMENT	8	62
7	COOPERATIVE DEVELOPMENT (TOSE'E TA'AVON)	GOVERNMENT	4	466
8	MASKAN (HOUSING) BANK	GOVERNMENT	26	1281
9	REFAH KARGARAN (WORKERS' WELFARE) BANK		3	1035
10	EQTESAD-E NOVIN (NEW ECONOMY) BANK		12	262

[17] Hamid Tehranifar, deputy director of the central bank: "The banks have about 500 to 600 companies, whose surplus must be sold during a specified period of time." (Mehr news agency, September 22, 2014). Ali Yazdani, deputy industry minister, said: "1,243 industrial and production units in industrial villages are now owned by banks" (ILNA news agency, April 20, 2016). And, in February 2014, Mohammad Nematzadeh, the minister of industry, mining and commerce said the units now under bank ownership have reached a total of 841.

	BANK NAME	AFFILIATION	NO. OF COMPANIES OWNED BY BANK	NO. OF BRANCHES
11	PARSIAN BANK	AFFILIATED WITH AUTO MANUFACTURERS WHOSE MAJORITY SHARES ARE OWNED BY **SETAD** AND THE IRGC	17	293
12	**KAR-AFARIN** (ENTREPRENEUR-SHIP) BANK	**SETAD** (KHAMENEI)	7	106
13	**SAMAN** (PROSPERITY) BANK		9	142
14	**PASARGAD** BANK	IRGC IS A SHAREHOLDER	68	327
15	**SARMAYEH** (CAPITAL) BANK		4	153
16	**SINA** BANK	**MOSTAZAFAN** FOUNDATION	3	242
17	**SHAHR** (CITY) BANK	TEHRAN MUNICIPALITY	14	261
18	**DEY** BANK	**SHAHID** FOUNDATION	13	91
19	**KHAVARMIANEH** (MIDDLE EAST) BANK		5	13
20	**ANSAR** BANK	IRGC	9	626
21	**SADERAT** (EXPORTS) BANK	IRGC IS A SHAREHOLDER	10	2706
22	**MELLAT** (PEOPLE) BANK	KHAMENEI'S **SETAD** IS A SHAREHOLDER	16	1592
23	**GARDESHGARI** (TOURISM) BANK	AHMADINEJAD FACTION	4	87
24	**QAVAMIN** BANK	STATE SECURITY FORCES (NAJA)	6	721
25	**TEJARAT** (COMMERCE) BANK	MAIN SHAREHOLDERS ARE THE IRGC AND THE **ASTAN-E QODS** FOUNDATION	21	2092
26	**IRAN ZAMIN**		5	356
27	**AYANDEH** (FUTURE) BANK			165
28	**IRAN AND VENEZUELA BANK**			
29	**HEKMAT IRANIAN BANK**	THE ARMY	2	128

	BANK NAME	AFFILIATION	NO. OF COMPANIES OWNED BY BANK	NO. OF BRANCHES
30	MEHR IRAN BANK			547
31	RESSALAT BANK	SALEHIN ECONOMIC GROUP		233

Sources: Parliament Research Center, June 2016 (for number of branches); Banker, September 13, 2014 (for number of companies owned by banks); various sources (for affiliation)

Secondly, the above-mentioned financial institutions and banks attracted deposits by taking advantage of government support and incentives.

Thirdly, these financial institutions and banks triggered an acceleration of liquidity at an astonishing pace and scale.

Fourthly, because of rampant inflation, the withdrawal of these deposits provided a mechanism to transfer a significant portion of the country's financial assets to the Supreme Leader's coffers. The rising inflation rate over the past decade has devalued people's deposits, but interest rates have not compensated for the devaluation. In reality, people's bank deposits gradually vanished in the face of the 50-60 percent inflation rate, while bank assets grew.

Fifthly, where did the wealth created through these mechanisms by financial and credit institutions and the banks go? Supported by Khamenei and on his orders in 2005, a small number of his IRGC affiliates and aides — who primarily ran foundations' economic activities as well as companies owned by Khamenei's office and the armed force — gained easy access to low-interest loans. According to the central bank, 29 percent of bank deposits have been loaned to just 173 applicants in the entire country.[5] Each of these applicants received loans valued at over $16 million. The majority of these loans have never been paid back to the banks, resulting in a financial crisis in its own right.

We can summarize the vicious cycle outlined above: The Supreme Leader's office uses its monopoly over firms to sell products and services at an inflated price. At the same time, it uses banks and financial instruments to seize a significant portion of the public wealth.

This is essentially what was done by the Allies to Iran's economy in the early 1940s. Mohammad-Ali Katouzian explains in his book, *The Political Economy of Iran*, that the Allies "effectively forced the Iranian government to put the country's resources at their disposal. The operation was carried out by means of monetary 'policy': in particular, the devaluation of the Iranian currency, the expansion of the money supply, and the extension of credit to Russia and Britain.

"Firstly, the Iranian currency was devalued by more than 100 percent. ... [This] reduced the earnings from the sale of her goods (or exports) to the Allies by almost half. ...

"Secondly, the fourfold expansion of the money supply ... was entirely inflationary ... to meet the Allies' local currency 'requirements,' enabling them to pay for their expenditures in the country.

"Thirdly, according to separate agreements with Britain and the Soviet Union, 60 percent of Iran's annual trade surplus with Britain, and the whole of the annual credit given to Russia were to be frozen until the end of the war. ... In plain language, the whole thing – the devaluation, the printing of money and the lending to Britain and Russia – was a case of armed robbery against a desperately weak and poor nation" (142-143).[18]

In 1953, Prime Minister Dr. Mohammad Mossaddeq, in his calculated and fact-based remarks in Parliament, estimated that since the invasion of Iran by the Allies in the early 1940s, prices had seen a ten-fold increase.[19]

One can draw parallels between the catastrophic economic cycle in Iran under the invasion of the Allies with a similar cycle under the theocratic rule of the *velayat-e faqih*. The devaluation of the currency, rising inflation, the burgeoning money supply, and provision of significant loans to the "occupiers" who never paid them back are common threads. Another important theme is the staggering scale of poverty and sheer misery inflicted on the Iranian people.

---

[18] Homa Katouzian, *The Political Economy of Modern Iran: Despotism and Pseudo-Modernism, 1926-1979*, Macmillan, 1981.

[19] H. Key-Ostovan, *The Politics of Negative Equilibrium in the Fourteenth Parliament* (in Farsi) (Tehran, Taban Press, 1946) .

ECONOMIC TRANSFORMATION BY SUBSIDY CUTS

HISTORIC EXAMPLE

In the view of many analysts, the implementation of the law to cut subsidies, which took effect in 2010, signaled the biggest economic transformation in Iran since the land reforms of 1962 instituted by Mohammad Reza Shah Pahlavi. There were many economists, both inside and outside of Iran, who surmised that this law, officially billed as a move towards free market commodity prices, would leave a positive mark on the Iranian economy. Disregarding the plan's backers within the corridors of power in Iran, other analysts who harbored optimism were perhaps unaware of the primary motives behind the *velayat-e faqih*'s fundamental political and economic decisions, which at their core focus on the survival of the regime and the protection of its exclusive security interests.

Iran's north-south railroad, the construction of which began in 1926, was primarily a function of Reza Shah's own narrow security interests: before all else, it was created to accelerate the movement of his armed forces to quell rebellions raging in southern Iran. His son's self-styled land reforms in the 1960s were first and foremost aimed at consolidating the monarchy's power. In the same manner, the current regime's elimination of subsidies aims to solidify the *velayat-e faqih's* domination over the economy in order to advance cardinal security interests of an isolated regime, not broad national interests.

It would be a mistake to assume that this strategy was one of Ahmadinejad's independent ideas. Much like the confiscation and seizure of economic institutions and efforts to dominate financial and monetary markets, the elimination of subsidies was made possible by Khamenei's direct intervention and unrelenting support. It was done to cast the country's economy as an engine to advance the *velayat-e faqih's* focused policies. A review of the disagreements between the government and the Parliament on the brink of the law's adoption shows that at every critical juncture, Khamenei intervened in favor of the law's adoption.[6]

EXPROPRIATING THE PEOPLE'S WEALTH THROUGH SUBSIDY CUTS

The elimination of subsidies, based on evidence amassed over the past five years, has not resulted in a buildup of the private sector; in fact, the opposite: When the price of gasoline increased 21-fold and the price of natural gas increased seven-fold, manufacturing costs sky-rocketed. In a bid to fend off the destructive impact of price hikes, the "Targeted Subsidies" bill mandated that 0.02 percent of the resulting revenues should be spent on supporting the manufacturing sector. This rhetoric, however, was never translated into action. Manufacturing facilities could not muster the strength to deal with rising prices because they could simply not compete with cheap imports. As a result, a large portion of production facilities, an estimated 60-70 percent, were either shut down or had their capacity reduced to less than a third. Their market share is now dominated by the *velayat-e faqih's* commercial enterprises, which after raising the required capital, are now flooding the market with imported products.

Meanwhile, the impact of the several-fold increase of the cost of fuel, gasoline, and utilities has dramatically diminished the real purchasing power of the consumer.

Thus, the elimination of subsidies has, in effect, channeled the wealth of the Iranian people to the Supreme Leader & Co. in two ways, while accelerating the monopolization of financial markets and broad-based economic activity: Firstly, by bringing about the annihilation of a large segment of the manufacturing sector; and secondly, through rampant inflation.

THE MEANS TO ONE END: SURVIVAL OF THE VELAYAT-E FAQIH

The three approaches mentioned above, namely the seizure and creation of economic powerhouses, the near-absolute control over financial markets, and the elimination of subsidies, are all means to a single end: the wholesale and sweeping seizure of public wealth and assets. The exact scale of the assets seized through these methods by Khamenei's office, the IRGC cooperatives and other armed forces is not entirely clear. There are no comprehensive, complete or credible accounts, only disparate reports and estimates regarding revenues attained from some of these activities. But, if we accept the premise that at least half of Iran's gross domestic product is generated through the financial and commercial activities of the *velayat-e faqih's* assortment of firms, foundations and financial and credit institutions, then we can simply infer the staggering annual revenues and profits filling their coffers.

On the other hand, over the past decade, the amount of capital accumulation in Iran has been negative or, in the most optimistic scenario, inconsequential.

WHERE DO THE PROFITS END UP?

Out of this sobering reality, a fundamental question arises: Where do the profits from the extensive seizure of the Iranian people's assets end up? It is true that some of these proceeds have been simply plundered or wasted through embezzlement, graft, and bad loans, and are generally laundered through the corrupt economic system that bears all the hallmarks of the *velayat-e faqih*. Yet the sweeping financial corruption represents only a meager portion of the astronomical profits made over the last decade. Therefore, one should look to other places and policies where the *velayat-e faqih* has parked these profits.

In one of his poems, the great Persian poet Rumi says, "If there's no thieving mouse inside our grain-store, then where's the wheat of forty years' hard work?"[20]

A "thieving mouse" has pillaged the "grain-store" that is the Iranian economy. It has wasted the country's wealth on domestic suppression, the nuclear program, and foreign military adventurism, especially in the conflicts of Syria, Yemen, and Iraq. Predictably, precise figures are hard to come by; the ruling regime has worked hard to hide the scale and methods of its financial gambits behind a thick veil of secrecy. Accountability and transparency regarding the expenditures of the *velayat-e faqih* on these destructive policies are nowhere to be found in the regime's laws, budget documents or

The regime's profits go to funding proxy wars and devastation in Yemen, Iraq, and Syria

---

[20] *The First Book of the Masnavi-ye Ma'navi.*

any official or unofficial text or financial report for that matter. It is abundantly clear that there is a willful cover-up policy to protect against leaks.

We can nevertheless conduct a restricted investigation by scrutinizing open sources, arguments and various calculations in order to reach something resembling a rational estimate.

COSTS OF THE WAR IN SYRIA

Profits from the regime's theft are used to fund prop up Assad's regime and perpetuate the Syrian civil war

Information on costs related to the Iranian regime's involvement in the war in Syria can be pieced together by combing through various media reports. Clearly, these reports, in and of themselves, do not supply a comprehensive or completely realistic account of the financial component in the *velayat-e faqih's* war policy. However, by compiling data from these reports,[7] and by factoring in other information — such as the fact that the monthly salaries of Shabia militia members are paid by the "*Emdad* (Aid) Committee"; that the monthly salaries of over 5,000 Jaish al-Shabi members are paid by

Khamenei's office; added to the fact that salaries for a significant portion of the Syrian army are paid by the IRGC; that Syria's military and logistical expenses are partially paid by Tehran; and that Iran's oil is exported to Syria at discounted prices — a conservative estimate for the cost of the war in Syria to the Iranian economy would be around $20B annually. It is estimated that over the course of the 5-year conflict in Syria, Tehran has spent between 80 to 100 billion dollars over the 5 years.

In addition, the Iranian regime pays salaries to foreign forces fighting in Syria, including its own IRGC personnel (8-10 thousand), Iraqi mercenaries working with the Qods Force (20 thousand), Afghans of the so-called Fatemiyoun (15-20 thousand),

SALARIES FOR THE MERCENARIES AND AGENTS IN SYRIA

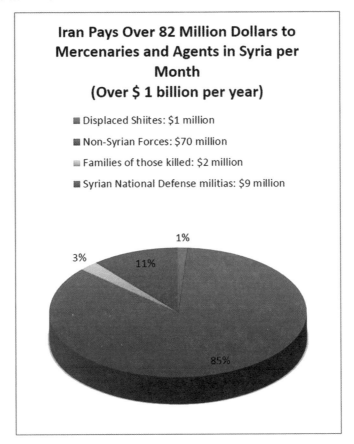

Iran Pays Over 82 Million Dollars to Mercenaries and Agents in Syria per Month
(Over $ 1 billion per year)

- Displaced Shiites: $1 million
- Non-Syrian Forces: $70 million
- Families of those killed: $2 million
- Syrian National Defense militias: $9 million

1%
3%
11%
85%

the Lebanese Hezbollah (7-10 thousand), and Pakistani forces of the so-called Zeinabiyoun (5-7 thousand). According to credible reports, the regime pays $1,550 to the IRGC's Iraqi mercenaries who are dispatched to Syria for a period of a month-and-a-half. If this figure is extrapolated for the 70,000-strong force under the command of the Iranian regime in Syria, then it can be estimated that Tehran pays $70,000,000 in salaries for non-Syrian forces involved in the conflict.

The Iranian regime also pays the salaries of the so-called Syrian National Defense militias. It is estimated that each member gets a monthly salary of about $100 to $200. Therefore, on average ($150 per person), and for a total of about 50,000 to 70,000 militia members tied to the IRGC in Syria, the Iranian regime pays out roughly $9,000,000 per month.

Tehran also pays families of its affiliates killed in Syria, including Syrian nationals, IRGC members, and its Iraqi, Lebanese and Afghan mercenaries. There have been over 10,000 casualties. The salaries paid to Syrian casualties are different from non-Syrians (Iranian, Afghan and Iraqi). Family members of slain Syrian forces receive roughly $40/month, while families of non-Syrian casualties receive a salary of about $500/month. If an average of $200 is considered for these casualties, the regime pays about $2,000,000 to the families of its forces killed during the Syrian conflict.

In addition to these expenses, Iran's clerical regime pays the displaced Shiites it protects after their forced expulsion or for those living in Shiite areas supported by the regime. For every family member, the regime pays roughly 4,000 Syrian Lira ($10). For example, in the cities of Nabl and al-Zahraa, the regime continued to pay money

Iranian foreign minister, Javad Zarif, meeting with Syrian President Bashar al-Assad in Damascus

to about 35,000 individuals for several years. The total number of Shiites who are protected by the Iranian regime exceeds 100,000 people. Therefore, Tehran pays about $1,000,000/month for these individuals.

As illustrated by the above figures, to advance its agenda in Syria, the Iranian regime is financially supporting over 250,000 people. These salaries amount to anywhere between $80,000,000 to $90,000,000 per month, or about one billion dollars over the course of a year.

Clearly, these salaries are only a small portion of the regime's overall expenses in Syria, and do not include the financial backing or the military and logistical support afforded to the Syrian army.

MEDDLING AND TERRORISM IN IRAQ

Iran's criminal profits also go to funding Shiite militias in Iraq

Since the ouster of former Iraqi Prime Minister Nouri al-Maliki, who was essentially Khamenei's puppet in Baghdad, the war and terrorism instigated by militias tied to the regime's Qods Force has expanded, in a bid to maintain the regime's political and military status. The Qods Force supplies a portion of the funds paid to these groups through a black-market economy run by its notorious commander Qassem Soleimani and the regime's ambassador in Iraq, Hassan Danaifar. Tehran is spending billions of dollars in Iraq to pursue its agenda. A significant portion of that money is provided by the IRGC, and its affiliate organizations, as well as entities associated with the Supreme Leader Khamenei.

THE WAR IN YEMEN

Iran funding Houthis in Yemen's war on the population

The war in Yemen, which has strategic import for the *velayat-e faqih,* has escalated since March 2015. The conflict has multiplied expenditures for Tehran, which supports the Ansar Allah Houthis. Prior to the start of the war, multiple reports surfaced about arms shipments, including ballistic missiles, from Iran to Houthi-controlled territories in Yemen. However, the impact on the Iranian economy of the war in Yemen remains unclear.

OTHER TERRORIST ACTIVITIES

Iran is also one of the major backers of Hamas

Added to these costs are the regime's extensive terrorist and fundamentalist activities elsewhere in the region, and primarily the costs of supporting the Lebanese Hezbollah, which has been involved in a full-scale war inside Syria since 2014. The Iranian regime's financial support to the group is estimated to be at least one billion dollars a year.[8]

Although the sums allocated to the regime's meddling and terrorism in other places are not comparable to those allocated to the current regional hotspots (Syria, Iraq or Yemen), still the significant amounts spent in Afghanistan, Bahrain and Palestine cannot be ignored. It is estimated, for example, that to date the regime has poured $1.3B into the coffers of Hamas alone.[21]

---

[21] Agence France Presse (AFP), November 12, 2013

THE NUCLEAR PROGRAM

The Iranian regime's nuclear program has been a remarkable burden on the Iranian economy. Several factors contributed to the ballooning of the program's costs, most notably intelligence operations to cover up the bulk of nuclear sites and activities, including building tunnels and bunkers deep inside mountains, creating parallel structures, and procuring the required contraband material, equipment and technology through western intermediaries.

Iran has maintained its nuclear weapons structure

The 2015 budget bill allocated the absurd amount of 8,460B Iranian rials ($267.6M) to Iran's Atomic Energy Organization. Needless to say, the real figures are strikingly different. International economists and reputable sources, as well as some of the regime's own former officials, have provided other estimates in this regard. A summary of these accounts can be seen in the endnotes.[9] Based on even the most conservative estimates, the regime's nuclear program has cost at least $10B a year for the past several decades.

THE MISSILE PROGRAM

Iran continues to test nuclear capable missiles

The regime's missile industry, which manufactures various missiles and regularly conducts tests, has incurred significant costs.[10] Contracts like the $11B agreement in 2009 by the IRGC to procure Intercontinental Ballistic Missiles (ICBMs) from North Korea, coupled with the building of several missile sites, provide a glimpse of these extraordinary expenditures. One must add the procurement of sensitive parts for missiles through the black market and the various cover-up operations. Still, these expenses all remain part of the hidden portions of the regime's military and security budget.

An Iranian missile, a product of Iran's multi billion dollar missile spending per year

ONGOING SECURITY, MILITARY AND FUNDAMENTALIST OPERATIONS

In the regime's annual budget bill, there are clear line items for the armed forces, intelligence and security agencies, state security forces, and special agencies charged with the export of terrorism and fundamentalism abroad. The same holds true for additional aid to unofficial agents of suppression. On top of these, the regime's institutions and forces dedicate a portion of the revenues they obtain from commercial and financial activities to their ongoing operations, as, for example, explicitly highlighted in the charter of the IRGC cooperative foundation.[22] However, the outlay required by these activities and the corresponding budget allocations are kept secret and cannot be independently assessed.

Iranian regime's military budget continues to rise

Therefore, we can only fall back on the official budget bill when it comes to the operating costs of the regime's security and armed forces. The table below shows the figures for recent years.

---

[22] Charter of the IRGC Cooperative Foundation

ESTIMATED BUDGET FOR MILITARY AND SECURITY AFFAIRS
(ALL FIGURES IN U.S. BILLION DOLLARS*)

CATEGORY	2008	2009	2010	2011	2012	2013	2014	2015
MILITARY	3.087	3.708	5.239	7.201	10.514	12.386	10.379	13.420
SECURITY	0.767	0.820	1.248	1.405	1.796	2.015	2.516	3.433
EXPORT OF FUNDAMENTALISM	0.507	0.604	0.661	0.731	0.983	1.042	1.081	1.407
SUPPORT FOR MEMBERS OF THE ARMED FORCES	0.799	0.958	1.704	1.508	2.280	3.407	3.480	3.440
SUPPORTING FOUNDATIONS AND ARMED FORCES COOPERATIVES	0.053	0.553	0.984	1.289	0.696	0.473	0.578	0.824
TOTAL	5.213	6.643	9.836	12.134	16.269	19.323	18.034	22.524
PERCENTAGE RELATIVE TO TOTAL BUDGET	17 PERCENT	22 PERCENT	24 PERCENT	22 PERCENT	31 PERCENT	29 PERCENT	24 PERCENT	30 PERCENT

* Exchange rate as of October 2016
Source: Official budget bills released by year. "Laws and Regulations Portal of the Islamic Republic of Iran", Presidential Legal Deputy, 2016. <http://www.dotic.ir/>

NOTE: The figures shown above have been mined from the general cost tables of the budget bills released by the regime over the past eight years. Although attempts have been made to logically categorize the scattered information in the various tables and lines of the budget bill to provide a more realistic account of the annual military and security budgets, undoubtedly this represents only a fraction of the reality and cannot account for all the military, security and terrorism expenses, which have been buried in various misleading and mislabeled lines in the government's annual budget.

The categories used in the above table (e.g. military, security, fundamentalism, etc.) are obviously not named as such in the regime's annual budget documents. The related figures that have been scattered in the various tables and lines of the regime's budget bill have been compiled and organized under the selected titles in our table. For example, the budget line items in the regime's bill for "rebuilding Afghanistan," "rebuilding holy shrines," "the al-Mostafa al-Alamiya Society," and the like have all been compiled under the rubric "export of fundamentalism." The *Emdad* Committee, which has as its official mandate aiding the poor, has also been included in the "export of fundamentalism" category. The next chapter details the real activities of this organization.

The budgets for the Ministry of Interior, the *Helal Ahmar* (Red Crescent) and the clerical *hawzas* (seminaries) have not been included in the table. A significant portion of these budgets are also allocated to domestic suppression and the export of terrorism abroad. For example, the regime's Red Crescent Society has offices in 23 (primarily African) countries, which use medical aid and charity as a cover to export fundamentalist or extremist ideologies.[23]

AN ECONOMY ALLOCATED TO TERRORISM, SUPPRESSION AND WARMONGERING

Despite the noted confines, the figures noted in the Estimated Budget for Military and Security Affairs Chart, guide us to several important conclusions:

Claims by the regime and its proponents abroad that the so-called defense budget is somewhere between 2 to 5 percent of the total budget are entirely inaccurate and baseless. Today, the actual amount is between 25 to 30 percent of the annual government budget. This figure is in addition to the much larger sums of money supplied by the foundations and cooperatives controlled by the regime's Supreme Leader.

The military and security portion of the budget relative to the public portion has increased from 17 percent in 2008 to roughly 30 percent in 2016. This rising trend is further proof of the hypothesis presented in this book, that the overhaul of the Iranian economy is geared towards ensuring the survival of the *velayat-e faqih* system.

---

[23] "Amir Mohsen Ziaii, the president of the Red Crescent Society detailed the society's activities in 30 medical services offices in other countries of the world. On the sidelines of meetings with 40 world ambassadors, he said at a news conference: The Islamic Republic Red Crescent Society has medical and aid offices in 23 countries around the world" (IRIB state-run broadcaster, November 11, 2015) .

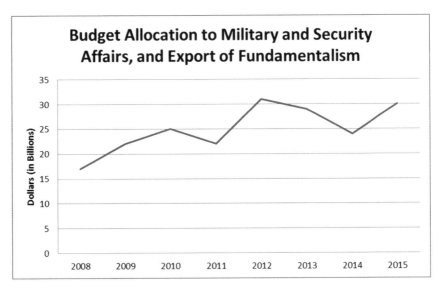

The table above shows a more realistic picture of the expenses allocated to suppression, terrorism, and warmongering. In 2015, the military and security costs, based on the exchange rate (to USD) indicated in this year's budget, were about $30B. The balance remaining for allocation to other sectors is roughly $58B.

2015 MILITARY, SECURITY AND TERRORISM BUDGET BROKEN DOWN BY CATEGORY

CATEGORY	DOLLARS (IN BILLIONS)
OFFICIAL COSTS IN GOVERNMENT BUDGET	$25
WAR IN SYRIA	$24
LEBANESE HEZBOLLAH	$1
NUCLEAR WEAPONS PROGRAM	$10
MISSILES PROGRAM	UNCLEAR
MEDDLING IN IRAQ	UNCLEAR
YEMENI HOUTHIS	UNCLEAR
TOTAL KNOWN FIGURES	$60

The critical conclusion that can be drawn from these calculations is that the attempt to ensure the survival of the *velayat-e faqih* system (even without considering the astronomical costs of the missile program and the wars in Iraq and Yemen) puts a $60B dent in the Iranian economy every year. That amount is much greater than the budget allocated to civic, non-military and non-security affairs. This circumstance is the result of the strategy implemented by Khamenei over a decade ago when he brought the Iranian economy under his firm control through "privatization" and "the elimination of subsidies."

IS THERE A PATH TO REFORM?

Now, let's return to a question posed earlier: Can the lifting of sanctions after the nuclear agreement in 2015 pull the Iranian economy back from the brink and reposition it on the path of reform? Much of what has already been said has provided the context for our answer. It does, however, bear repeating that since the very survival of the *velayat-e faqih* system depends on devouring the country's economic resources as well as a relentless confiscation of assets and revenues, there can be no conceivable genuine economic reforms under this theocracy. Real reforms would lead only to the collapse of the pillars on which the regime rests, and thereby it's entire structure.

The definitive conclusion is that without the removal of the *velayat-e faqih* system in its entirety and without the establishment of democracy in the political arena, the woes and maladies of the Iranian economy cannot be cured in earnest. That is why the economic policies of the Rouhani government cannot align with real and genuine reforms. The orientation of the budgets during Rouhani's tenure (since 2013) has remained the prioritization of military and security imperatives. This fact, coupled with Rouhani's remarkable statements that point to the five-fold increase of "strengthening of the defensive structures" through government activities,[24] confirm that Rouhani's policies have not departed from the policies of the past. Rouhani has neither the ability nor the will to implement genuine reforms. Reform is essentially incompatible with their political objectives, because it would also diminish their own political power and status.

At the same time, the regime's inherent antagonism to real reforms, which for a long time has protected it against various fissures and ruptures, is now threatening the entire edifice of the ruling system.

---

[24] Hassan Rouhani: "Some say that the government is thinking about the economy, reducing inflation, overcoming recession, medical care, health and foreign policy. They say that the government does not want to strengthen the defense backbone. I must say that we have done so much in terms of strategic weapons and strengthening the defense backbone in just the past two years, that it would be tantamount to 80 percent of what was done over the previous decade." (State-run Channel 1 TV, August 3, 2015).

FROM "SYNERGY" TO DISINTEGRATION

The political economy of the past decade has been transformed around the principle of striking a degree of "synergy" between power and wealth. The term "synergy" has been repeatedly used in the documents that formulated the regime's general policies over the past decade. Its use in that context does not convey the true definition of the term (i.e. "a mutually advantageous conjunction or compatibility of distinct business participants or elements"[25]); rather, it is used as a rationale to monopolize and take full control of all the levers of power and wealth generation. This book refers to that phenomenon as "closing ranks" or "contraction," which may be more in line with the true characteristics of the peculiar *velayat-e faqih* system.

In the period after the watershed moment of 2005, Khamenei accelerated the interaction between his powers and authorities in the ruling elite, the export of terrorism and fundamentalism to regional countries, and among all economic activities under his control. The ascent to power of Nouri al-Maliki as prime minister in Iraq and Mahmoud Ahmadinejad as president in Iran, and the devouring of large portions of the Iranian economy were tangible, concrete consequences of this policy. Without doubt, Khamenei thus mustered the financial capacity to advance domestic suppression and his agenda to dominate the region. Without the financial resources resulting from these "synergies," the regime's regional meddling could not have been implemented on the scale achieved.

Khamenei was also able to marginalize the main rival faction within the regime. He prevented the growth of the private sector, which, according

The minister of Intelligence identified the private sector as a threat to the regime

[25] Merriam-Webster Dictionary.

to Heydar Moslehi, the Minister of Intelligence at the time, could have threatened the regime.[26] And, to a large extent, thanks to the domination of the IRGC and its foundations over firms and factories, Khamenei was able to suppress protests by workers and employees.

But after a series of accelerated measures, the "synergy" initiative has forced the entire ruling structure into a period of attrition:

From a political standpoint, the 2009 uprisings represented the first and the most important rupture in the ruling regime. The subsequent series of fissures, all of which impacted the center of power (velayat-e faqih), expanded the erosion: Ahmadinejad, Khamenei's protégé, rebelled against his boss[11]; the unified coalition of fundamentalists effectively collapsed[12], the marginalized rival faction returned to power spelling defeat for the policy of contraction[13], the client government of Maliki was ousted in Iraq[14], Syria became embroiled in crises[15], the regime's reach in Yemen was reduced[16], and Khamenei retreated from a strategic indicator of power, namely the project to manufacture a nuclear weapon.[17]

From an economic standpoint, major economic indicators over the past decade point to a disastrous trend.

The table below, which relies on official statistics, gives a glimpse of this collapse:

YEAR	INFLATION RATE (PERCENT)	ECONOMIC GROWTH (PERCENT)	PER CAPITA INCOME ($)	CAPITAL GROWTH (PERCENT)	MONEY SUPPLY (IN BILLIONS OF DOLLARS)	SOCIAL WELFARE (PERCENT)	INCOME GROWTH (PERCENT)
2005	10.4	5.7	$6,924	4.7	$29B	11	7.7
2006	11.9	6.2	$7,243	-1.4	$41B	5	5.7
2007	18.4	6.9	$8,232	11.1	$52B	9	3.2
2008	25.4	0.8	$7,849	11	$61B	1	-4.3
2009	10.8	3	$7,403	2.9	$75B	-7	8.4
2010	12.4	6.5	$8,073	3.8	$94B	11	2.3
2011	21.5	4.3	$8,488	3.5	$112B	6	-10.3
2012	30.5	-6.8	$6,892	-23.8	$147B	-19	-9.6
2013	34.7	-1.9	$6,605	-6.9	$190B	-6	-7.3

Source: Iranian Central Bank, National Iranian Accounts, January 2015.

---

[26] Heydar Moslehi, former intelligence minister during Ahmadinejad's second term in office speaking at the *Police and Security Conference 1404*, November 2011.

The figures in the above table are based on official statistics released by the regime's Central Bank, the most prevalent official source of data for economic affairs. These statistics are by nature extremely conservative. For example, the table puts the inflation rate in the years 2010 to 2013 at 11 percent to about 35 percent (at its height). Independent experts believe that the average rate of inflation throughout this period did not fall below 50 percent.

The above table nevertheless leads us to several important conclusions: Firstly, over the past decade:

- ☑ The GDP has fallen by 12 percent

- ☑ Per capita income has fallen by a third

- ☑ Not only has there been no generation of new capital, but also there has been a 24 percent contraction

- ☑ The supply of money has grown 6.5 times

- ☑ Social welfare has been reduced by 30 percent

- ☑ Inflation has increased by 176 percent, while total income levels throughout have been reduced by 4 percent

- ☑ Over 64 percent of private sector assets have been lost. In other words, the *velayat-e faqih* has seized 64 percent of the entire base of Iranian society.

Another important indicator is the rate of unemployment. The Central Bank figures depart significantly from reality. According to some of the regime's most senior economic officials, the number of jobs created in these years has been the lowest in the past 50 years. In 2012, Iranian society saw a net loss in the number of jobs.[18]

Finally, we must also point to the "water crisis,"[27] "water refugees," "wasted farmlands," and "dried up lakes and wetlands,"[28] all of which have led to the collapse of agriculture. The dramatic reduction in water levels across Iran is one of the important developments of the period under study. It would be a mistake to reduce the causes of these developments to things like mismanagement, unruly digging

---

[27] As drought grips Iran, farmers lament loss of a way of life, Los Angeles Times, September 28, 2016; http://www.latimes.com/world/la-fg-iran-drought-snap-story.html

[28] Dying Lake Urmia reflects a broader problem in Iran, Los Angeles Times, March 21, 2014; http://www.latimes.com/world/middleeast/la-fg-iran-lake-20140321-story.html

Lake Urmia, once one of the world's largest salt lakes, has almost completely dried

of wells, construction of too many dams, theft or corruption. These factors were certainly in play and have had a destructive impact in their own right. Their effects, however, were primarily caused by the *velayat-e faqih's* overall strategy, which has utilized the environmental assets of the country, and water as a core resource, to ensure the survival of the regime. Studies show that the large-scale initiatives redirecting rivers, building dams or erecting structures have by and large been a function of the expansion of the nuclear program or plans that have been in one way or another related to the IRGC's security and military interests.

This widespread destruction is not the result of simply "mistakes"; rather, it results from a willful calculation to ensure the survival of a regime that has brought about the collapse of the country's natural resources; a strategy that is contradictory to the natural and historical development of Iranian society. Ironically, it is this very contradiction that will spell the end for the regime.

Secondly, as the official statistics (above table) show, the economic crises in Iran, which began in 2008, reached their height in 2012. The acceleration in the devaluation of the country's currency, the Rial, began in 2010, while the international oil embargo began in 2012. Therefore, although the sanctions played a major part in forcing Khamenei to retreat from his nuclear ambitions, they were not the cause of the economic collapse, serving only as a catalyst. In fact, the sanctions brought to the surface the remarkable vulnerabilities of the regime's economy, to the extent that just a year-and-a-half after the oil embargo, the regime accepted the Geneva deal in November 2013. If the "synergy" strategy had actually strengthened the *velayat-e faqih*, either from a political or financial position, Tehran would have never retreated from its nuclear ambitions.

Thirdly, it would be a mistake to think that the profound misery resulting from the economic conditions and the fall in living standards only impact the impoverished sectors of Iranian society, while leaving the rulers immune from fundamental threats thanks to their endless stream of petrodollars. The economic malaise before 1979 was one of the factors that contributed to the fall of the Shah, even though the depth and breadth of the Shah's troubles were much less than the plight of the current ruling mullahs.

A REGIME LEFT ISOLATED AND UNSTABLE

Today, the *velayat-e faqih* regime has effectively marginalized or eliminated the private sector, shrunk the middle class, pushed university graduates out of the labor market, confiscated major portions of public assets, and consolidated almost all of the economy in the hands of a few. It has, as such, upset its own strategic balance, losing its base for political stability. In other words, Tehran finds itself in the most vulnerable position to date.

What this means is that the regime's "synergy" strategy, which has linked political and economic power more closely than ever before in Iran, will prove its own undoing and erode the ruling regime's power. Although there are fundamental historical differences between the conditions prevailing during the *Safavid* dynasty in the 1500s and the *velayat-e faqih's* circumstances today, it may prove illuminating to cite an example about the conditions that led to that dynasty's downfall when the "synergy" of power and wealth peaked.

In his book, "The Politics of Iran," James Bill writes, "In his valuable study, *Turkestan Down to the Mongol Invasion*, V.V. Barthold writes: 'Throughout the whole system of the Eastern Muslim political organization there runs like a red thread the division of all the organs of the administration into two main categories, the dargah (palace) and the diwan (chancery). [29] In Safavi times, this division (*khassah* and *divan*) was an integral part of the administration and it played a major role in both the rise and decline of the system. These two forces were in constant tension with one another and in the end this tension snapped as the *khassah* absorbed and digested the functions and power of the *divan*. It was at this time that the Safavi system crumbled.'"[30]

Similarly, the current regime's Supreme Leader has gone all out, grabbing all the levers of political and economic power. But, the monopolization that initially brought destruction and horrendous effects for Iranian society now sets the stage for the downfall of the illegitimate ruling system itself.

---

[29] See Barthold, *Turkestan Down to the Mongol Invasion*, 2d ed. (London: Oxford University Press, 1928), p 227.

[30] James Alban Bill, *The Politics of Iran: Groups, Classes and Modernization* (Charles E. Merrill Publishing Co, 1972), p34.

THE NEW ECONOMIC STRUCTURE: A MIND-BOGGLING CONGLOMERATE OF 14 POWERHOUSES

A rticle 44 of the Iranian regime's Constitution states: "The economy of the Islamic Republic of Iran is to consist of three sectors: state, cooperative, and private, and is to be based on systematic and sound planning."[31] However, as noted earlier, in his 2005 order, Khamenei announced a new structure to consist of cooperatives, and private and non-government public sectors. During the transfer of state-owned assets, a remarkable portion went to the "non-government public sector," and the ownership and management of Iran's economic powerhouses took on a new form.

Two years after the publication of Khamenei's order, the parliament adopted a bill entitled "management of agricultural services," wherein the non-government public sector is defined as follows: "A non-government public institution or entity is a specific organization that enjoys legal independence and has been or will be established based on the approval of the Islamic Consultative Council (Parliament), that has an annual budget more than 50 percent of which is funded through non-government resources, and that carries out activities and services of a public nature."

In practice, however, this newly branded sector is the business juggernaut controlled by the office of the *velayat-e faqih*, and is comprised of the armed forces, foundations (*bonyads*), and institutions specifically charged with advancing the regime's policies of suppression and export of terrorism. The new economic landscape, a culmination of the most important political and economic shift of the last decade, has been founded on the unbridled and unrivaled expansion of the so-called "public sector." It has transformed the *velayat-e faqih* into the main employer in the country in place of the government.

To convey an overview of the new formation of the Iranian economy under the rule of the *velayat-e faqih*, a list of institutions tied to each of the regime's entities and armed forces, as well as their sub-components, has been provided in subsequent sections of this manuscript. The list does not include some of the other *bonyads* and entities whose assets are more limited, among them: Astan-e Hazrat Massoumeh, Shah Cheragh, Shah Abdol-Azim, the Islamic Propaganda Organization, *Sodouq-e Bozorg* Foundation, Al-

---

[31] Constitution of the Islamic Republic of Iran, Official Website of the Islamic Republic of Iran Permanent Mission to the United States, www.iran-un.org/en/constitution, Article 44.

Zahra Society, *15-Khordad* Foundation, *Zeynab Kobra* Foundation, and the Islamic Revolution Housing (*Maskan*) Foundation. Also excluded are the 13 companies of the Defense Department: Electronic Industry Parts and Equipment, Iz Iran, Shiraz Electronic Industries, SA Iran Telecommunications, Esfahan Optics, Iran Electronic Industries, Aerospace Organization, Air Industries Organization, Iran Air Industries Corporation, Iran Aircraft Renewal and Support, Iran Airplane Manufacturing Industries, Qods Air Industries, and Medical Services Organization for Armed Forces Personnel.

The following pages list in 14 separate sections the foundations controlled by the *velayat-e faqih*. The content and details have been compiled from press reports and the regime's official statistics and documents regarding these institutions. Although this long list of companies is mindboggling and hard to follow, we can assume with certainty that the number listed still falls short of the many more entities, companies, and financial institutions that are controlled by the Supreme Leader's office and his affiliates.

1 – SETAD-E EJRAIY-E FARMAN-E HAZRAT-E EMAM

Setad-e Ejraiy-e Farman-e Haz-rat-e Emam or Headquarters for Executing the Order of the Imam (the U.S. Treasury Department refers to this entity as The Execution of Imam Khomeini's Order 'EIKO'), herein referred to as *Setad,* is the richest and highest revenue-generating enterprise controlled by Khamenei. On June 4, 2013, the Treasury Department subjected this entity and 37 of its associate entities to sanctions pursuant to Executive Order 13599, which blocks the property of the Government of Iran.[32]

Setad's influence and domination over the Iranian economy surpass even that of the Islamic Revolutionary Guard Corps (IRGC). It is the most assertive of the so-called "non-government public sector" companies when it comes to the confiscation of assets. An important difference between *Setad* and other similar institutions in the sphere of the *velayat-e faqih's* influence is that it has been able to take possession of some of the most profitable and largest commercial and financial firms, thanks to the direct and daily backing of Khamenei himself.

A Reuters investigation published in 2013[33] estimated *Setad* assets to be worth around $95 billion. Those assets not mentioned in the Reuters report, but listed below, reveal the wealth of *Setad* to be much more than this estimate. In reality, *Setad* is the engine of

---

[32] Treasury Targets Assets of Iranian Leadership; https://www.treasury.gov/press-center/press-releases/Pages/jl1968.aspx

[33] Steve Stecklow, Babak Dehghanpisheh and Yeganeh Torbati, "Assets of the Ayatollah, the Economic Empire Behind Iran's Supreme Leader," Reuters news agency, November 11, 2013. See: http://www.reuters.com/investigates/iran/#article/part1

Khamenei's "synergy" strategy for the Iranian economy.

The mandate of the *"Tadbir Energy Development Group"*, one member of the *Setad* conglomerate, is "to establish a powerful international oil, gas, petrochemical and energy producer through the creation or ownership of effective shares of active companies or companies with potentially viable assets."

A review of *Setad's* activities also confirms that this complex is one of the most important interlocutors for transactions with western companies. For example, in the conclusion

Supreme Leader Khamenei is the direct overseer of Setad, an organization with assets worth approximately $95 billion

of this text, mention is made of some of the deals involving the pharmaceutical components of *Setad* with French, American, British, Italian and Swiss companies.

The new administrative organ of *Setad* has 100 employees, and is authorized to make policy and supervise the institution's activities. The members of this board are handpicked by Khamenei himself. They include the likes of mullah Hossein-Ali Nayyeri,[34] a judge during the 1988 massacre of thousands of political prisoners; Hossein Shariatmadari,[35] an interrogator, torturer and now Khamenei's representative in the state-run daily *Kayhan*; and Mohammad Mohammadi Golpayegani, Khamenei's chief of staff.[36]

To strengthen the financial backbone of *Setad*, in 2010, Khamenei transferred close to $1B worth of assets from Astan-e Abdol-Azim in Rey city to *Setad*.

The names of some of the parent companies within this conglomerate are:

---

[34] http://www.iranfocus.com/en/index.php?option=com_content&view=article&id=30713

[35] http://www.nytimes.com/2007/09/22/world/middleeast/22shariamadari.html

[36] https://www.stratfor.com/analysis/special-series-iranian-intelligence-and-regime-preservation

• THE TADBIR ENERGY DEVELOPMENT GROUP

The Tadbir Energy Development Group,[37] also sanctioned under Iranian Transactions and Sanctions Regulations by the U.S. Treasury Department,[38] has the following holdings:

TADBIR ENERGY DEVELOPMENT HOLDING COMPANY: This enterprise is active in the exploration and production of oil and gas, refineries, petrochemicals and other commercial pursuits. It has been reported that the so-called "Peace" pipeline project in Pakistan, a deal worth about $500M, belongs to this holding. 80 percent of another project to build a refinery in Hormoz, as well as the Mansouri oil field development have also been awarded to this holding. Its subsidiaries include:

- Pars Oil[39] (75.6 percent)
- Commercial Pars Oil (100 percent)
- Northern Drilling (10 percent)
- Persia Oil and Gas[40] (100 percent) – Its first contract, worth about $600M, was to develop the Yaran oil field.
- Chemical Managers (100 percent)
- Bahman Geno Company (formerly Hormoz Oil Refinery) (80 percent)
- Parsian Tadbir Refinery (80 percent)
- Qaed Basir Petrochemicals[41] (80 percent)
- Abadan Electrical Production Company (75 percent)
- Tadbir Drilling (100 percent)
- Rey Power (Rey Niru Engineering Company)[42] (100 percent)

MOBIN IRAN ELECTRONICS EXPANSION HOLDING COMPANY

- Telecommunications (19 percent)
- Etemad Mobin Development Company

---

[37] http://www.tadbirenergy.com

[38] https://sanctionssearch.ofac.treas.gov/Details.aspx?id=5790

[39] http://www.parsoilco.com

[40] http://www.pogidc.com

[41] http://www.gbpc.net

[42] http://www.reyniroo.com

- Talia (mobile phone operator), a portion of which was purchased by Mobin Iran in 2012
- Mobin Society Communications
- Mobin 1
- Mobile Communications Company – This company provides mobile services; a portion of it belongs to the IRGC Cooperative.

TADBIR INDUSTRY AND MINING DEVELOPMENT HOLDING COMPANY

BARKAT PHARMACEUTICALS HOLDING COMPANY: This parent company owns 60.6 percent of the Alborz Investment Group, the second-largest pharmaceutical holding company in the country. Companies in this conglomerate include:

- Alborz Pharmaceuticals Company
- Sobhan Pharmaceuticals Company (manufactures pills)
- Iran Pharmaceuticals Company
- Tolid Pharmaceuticals Company
- Sobhan Oncology Company – Manufactures Paclitaxel, licensed by the Swiss pharmaceutical company Stragen.
- KBC (importer)
- Alborz Distributors
- Alborz Ascend Investment Company
- Alborz Balak Company
- Farabi Pharmaceutical Manufacturer (17 percent)
- Razak Pharmaceutical Manufacturer (12 percent)
- Ati Farmed Company (51 percent)
- BioSun Company (20 percent)
- Alborz-Zagros Company

TADBIR STRATEGIC STUDIES AND MANAGEMENT CONSULTANT GROUP

TADBIR CONSTRUCTION DEVELOPMENT COMPANY: This holding company, also sanctioned under Iranian Transactions and Sanctions Regulations by the U.S. Treasury Department, manages construction for residential, commercial and tourist projects.[43] It has four large construction companies under its umbrella.

• SETAD ASSET AND PROPERTY ORGANIZATION

This organization has confiscated real estate properties, land, assets, residential homes, heritage and historic properties, and many others, especially over the past decade.

• THE FINANCIAL MARKET

- Mellat Insurance[44] (15 percent)

- Kar-Afarin Bank (11 percent)

- Parsian Bank (16 percent) – This bank's main shareholder is Iran-Khodro auto manufacturer. *Setad* also owns shares in Iran-Khodro.

- Tadbir Investments – This holding company is active in the stock market, the financial market and securities. It owns six other companies.

• OTHERS

- Iran Khodro[45] (5 percent)

- Rey Investment Company

- Mobin Iran Company

- Modaber Investment Company

- Barkat Foundation – Barkat calls itself a charity organization, and operates as such on the surface. However, this is a front company hiding astronomical profits for *Setad*.

---

[43] https://sanctionssearch.ofac.treas.gov/Details.aspx?id=5789

[44] http://www.mellatinsurance.com

[45] http://www.ikco.ir/en/

2. BONYAD-E MOSTAZAFAN

The Islamic Revolution *Mostazafan* (oppressed) Foundation operates under the direct supervision of Khamenei, who hand-picks its president.[46] In 1997, Mohsen Rafiqdoost, the foundation's former president, said the *Mostazafan* Foundation owned 400 commercial companies, and produced 28 percent of textiles, 22 percent of cement, about 45 percent of non-alcoholic beverages, 28 percent of tires, and 25 percent of sugar produced in Iran.[47]

The Ministry of Roads and Urban Development announced on November 1, 2016, that it had awarded another massive development project to the *Mostazafan* Foundation. Mahmoud Navidi, managing director of "Khomeini Airport Estates Company" announced that the Ministry will sign a contract with the *Mostazafan* Foundation for construction and operation of the "Salam Terminal in Khomeini Airport" in Tehran. The state-run ILNA news agency, quoting Navidi, wrote: "This project was awarded to the *Mostazafan* Foundation without competitive bidding. According to [Navidi], the contract was awarded upon the recommendation and approval of Rouhani's cabinet."

The Foundation's investment in this project was announced at $4B USD. Construction of part of the Salam Terminal had previously been awarded to the National Construction Company, a subsidiary of the *Mostazafan* Foundation.[48]

Some of the other main subsidiaries of this foundation are listed below.

---

[46] http://irmf.ir/En/

[47] "A Cooperative Called the Mostazafan," *Rah-e Sabz*, In Farsi <http://www.rahesabz.net/story/18778>

[48] Statement of the National Council of Resistance of Iran, NCRI, "Taxpayers' Money Looted by Giant 'Revolutionary Foundations' via Rouhani," November 5, 2016.

HOLDING COMPANIES:

Alavi Foundation

THE PEYVAND FERDOUS PARS AGRICULTURE AND GARDENING, which includes: Sirjan Bonyad Agriculture, Mashhad Gardening and Farming, Pars Milk And Meat Investment, Fajre Esfahan, Fajre Sari Gardening and Agriculture, Dasht-e Naz-e Sari Farming, Sina Seed and Plant, Ebrahim Abad Agriculture, Ferdous Tehran Agriculture and Gardening, Peyvand-e Khavaran Agro Industry, Nemat Agro Industry, Golcheshmeh Agro Industry, Ran-e Behshahr Agriculture and Farm Animals, and Mahya Agro Industry.

KAVEH PARS MINING INDUSTRY DEVELOPMENT

PARS MILK AND BEEF INVESTMENTS which includes: Magsal Agro and Farm Animals, Teliseh Nemooneh Farm Animals, Milk and Farm Animals, Yassouj Agro, Mahdashe Sari Milk and Beef, Azarnegin Agro Industry, Binaloud Neyshabour Agro Industry, Dasht-e Novin Malayer Agro Industry, Negin Fam Khouzestan Agro Industry, Arak Cultivation, Kangavar Beef and Milk, Zagros Shahr-e Kord Milk and Beef, Khorramdareh Agro Industry.

ALAVI URBANIZING AND ENGINEERING SERVICES

SINA PAYA SANAT DEVELOPMENT (GENERAL INDUSTRY)

SINA ENERGY DEVELOPMENT

SABA POWER AND ENERGY INDUSTRIES

PAYA SAMAN PARS INVESTMENT

IRAN HOUSING DEVELOPMENT

SINA INVESTMENT MANAGEMENT

PARSIAN TOURISM AND RECREATION CENTERS

SINA COMMUNICATIONS AND TECHNOLOGIES

SINA FOOD INDUSTRIES DEVELOPMENT which includes: Domestic Chickens, Oroumieh Toyour Complex, Mehrshar Food Industry, Pakdis, Behnoush Iran, Ab-Ali Beverages, Shahd-e Kouhrang, Glucosan, Gousht-Iran, Pak Dairy Products.

POUSHAN PARS INVESTMENTS

PARS CELLULOSE AND WOOD INVESTMENTS

KAVEH PARS MINING INDUSTRY

ALAVI ENGINEERING AND URBAN DEVELOPMENT

PANID PARS SUGAR INVESTMENT

RAHNEGAR PARS INVESTMENT MANAGEMENT

ATIEH SAZAN PLAN MANAGEMENT

ZAMZAM COMPANY

CULTURAL INSTITUTIONS:

BONYAD MUSEUMS CULTURAL INSTITUTION

NOVIN DANESHMAND RESEARCH & DEVELOPMENT INSTITUTE

IRANIAN CONTEMPORARY HISTORICAL STUDIES

TABAN LIGHT CINEMA

OTHER COMPANIES:

SHAHID MOTAHHARY AGRICULTURE & INDUSTRY

TEHRAN SHOMAL FREEWAY

TEHRAN CEMENT

BEHRAN OIL

BAYANAT HADI AUDIT AND INSPECTION

FINANCIAL INSTITUTIONS:

SINA BANK (270 BRANCHES)

AYANDEH (FUTURE) CREDIT AND FINANCIAL INSTITUTION

SINA FINANCIAL AND INVESTMENTS COMPANY

3. ASTAN-E QODS-E RAZAVI

The Astan-e Qods-e Razavi Foundation has been called an unbridled giant when it comes to Iran's political economy.[49] It is the largest employer in the northeastern province of Khorasan. It has control over (more than 50 percent ownership) in at least 58 large companies. It also owns significant shares in 31 other companies. These include financial institutions and brokers, hospitals, media outlets, publishing houses, animal husbandry, Internet service companies, and car manufacturers, among many others.

According to websites affiliated with the economic organization of this institution, the Razavi economic organization is recognized as the biggest economic holding in eastern Iran with high diversity in different businesses. It controls the production of 10 percent of sugar, 11 percent of decorative stones, 3.7 percent of city and inter-city coach buses, and one-sixth of bread production in the country.[50]

The cartel of companies tied to Astan-e Qods-e Razavi controls the annual production of 47,000 tons of non-homogenized milk, 2,000 tons of red meat, 1,000 tons of white meat, 100,000 tons of agricultural products, 10,000 square meters of fabric, 6,000 square meters of hand-weaved carpets, while also executing over 136 construction, development, road and urban development projects.

Large swathes of farm land in northeastern Iran, estimated to be at least 990,000 acres with an estimated value of over $20B, are owned by this foundation. Additionally, 43.5 percent of Mashhad city's urban land is under the foundation's ownership. It also has endowments in 14 provinces, real estate offices in 20 provinces, and 300,000 rentals.

---

[49]   http://www.aqr.ir/Portal/Home/Default.aspx

[50]   http://en.reorazavi.org/

In the context of the regime's export of fundamentalism, the foundation conducts activities in Syria, including bridge construction. In 2016, the foundation and the IRGC conducted negotiations for the foundation to allocate at least 20 percent of its annual income to cover the IRGC's expenses.

Below is a list of some of the conglomerate's firms and holding companies.

HOLDING COMPANIES:

CONSTRUCTION

- Qods Razavi Concrete and Machinery Construction Company
- Qods Razavi Residential and Construction Company
- Astan-e Qods Razavi Engineering and Urban Development Consultants
- Qods Razavi Water and Soil Engineering Company
- Qods Razavi Light Structure Manufacturers

AUTO MANUFACTURING

- Shahab Automobile Company
- Shahab Transportation Company
- Combine Manufacturing

FOOD PRODUCTS

- Qods Razavi Flour Company
- Razavi Leaven Company
- Razavi Food Products Company
- Razavi Dairy Products Company
- Qods Razavi Bread Company

SUGAR INDUSTRY

- Abkouh Sugar Company
- Torbat Heydarieh Sugar Company
- Chenaran Sugar Company

AGRICULTURAL

- Razavi Agriculture
- Chenaran Agriculture and Endowments
- Esfarayen Agro Industry
- Anabed Agro Industry
- Sarakhs Agro Industry
- Astan Qods Razavi Land Institution
- Nemouneh Farm Agro Industry Institution
- South Khorasan Endowment and Agriculture Institution
- Semnan Endowment and Agriculture Institution

TEXTILE INDUSTRY

- Astan-e Qods Razavi Carpet Production Company
- Khosravi Weaving and Textile Company

RAZAVI INFORMATION AND COMMUNICATION TECHNOLOGIES HOLDING COMPANY

PHARMACEUTICALS

- Thamen Pharmaceuticals

FINANCIAL

- Razavi Credit Union
- Razavi Brokerage

OTHERS

- Razavi Oil and Gas
- Astan-e Qods Razavi Wood Industries
- Qods Razavi Mining Company
- Sarakhs Special Economic Region
- Qods Razavi Livestock (over 130,000 cows)
- Razavi Islamic Sciences University
- Imam Reza University

4. BONYAD-E SHAHID (MARTYR)

The *Shahid* (Martyr) Foundation was created in 1979 on the orders of former Supreme Leader Ruhollah Khomeini.[51] Its reach grew after the start of the eight-year Iran-Iraq war in the 1980s, as it provided services to the victims' families. Much like other similar institutions, the foundation took huge leaps in the 1990s to accumulate wealth quickly. Under Khamenei's direct control, the foundation took ownership of many financial, commercial and manufacturing enterprises. Despite owning a vast range of assets and generating significant revenues, it is also allocated a portion of the government budget. The chairman of the foundation is a representative of the Supreme Leader.

The U.S. Department of the Treasury designated the Martyrs Foundation on July 24, 2007 under Executive Order 13224. Designations under E.O. 13224 freeze any assets the designees may have under U.S. jurisdiction and prohibit transactions by U.S. persons with the designees. In its statement, Treasury said, "The Martyrs Foundation is an Iranian parastatal organization that channels financial support from Iran to several terrorist organizations in the Levant, including Hizballah, Hamas, and the Palestinian Islamic Jihad (PIJ). To this end, the Martyrs Foundation established branches in Lebanon staffed by leaders and members of these same terrorist groups. Martyrs Foundation branches in Lebanon have also provided financial support to the families of killed or imprisoned Hizballah and PIJ members, including suicide bombers in the Palestinian territories."[52]

---

[51] http://www.isaar.ir/

[52] Twin Treasury Actions Take Aim at Hizballah's Support Network, U.S. Treasury Department, July 24, 2007; https://www.treasury.gov/press-center/press-releases/Pages/hp503.aspx

Some of the companies and institutions controlled by the *Shahid Foundation* are listed below.

KOWSAR ECONOMIC ORGANIZATION, which itself owns over 30 companies, including:

- Sobhan Investments
- Tehran Electric
- Namad Kowsar Food Industry Investments
- Kowsar Agricultural Investments, which owns 24 companies
- Kowsar Mining and Industrial Development Investments (whose portfolio of mines has grown to 10,000 kilometers since 2015)
- Kowsar Power and Electronics Investment
- Kowsar Agricultural Mechanization and Industrial Development
- Moin Kowsar Construction and Builders Investment
- Kowsar Credit Union. According to the financial institution itself, in 2015 its assets were worth over $4.1B.
- *Zakhireh Shahed* Investments owns 10 companies whose activities range from construction, energy production, and commerce to airport services. The company started back in 1984 with a few thousand dollars given by Khomeini.
- Agricultural Industry Development Services (in Zanjan)
- Khorasan Cotton and Cooking Oil
- *Shahed* University
- Imam Khomeini Technical Center
- *Shahed* Charity Fund

DEY BANK (47 BRANCHES): According to the Dey Bank's financial disclosure information for fiscal year 2014, the bank owns over $3.5B worth of assets; additionally, it owns at least 13 other companies, including:

- Didar Development Company
- Dey Electronic Commerce Company
- Dey Atieh Sazan Company
- Dey Brokerage
- Dey Insurance
- Dey Leasing
- Bou-Ali Investment Company
- Gostar Fardad Commerce
- Dey Currency Exchange
- Dey Bank Investments
- Royay-e Rouz Kish Company
- Abadi Residential Builders
- Iranian Dey Financial Services

5. EMDAD (RELIEF) COMMITTEE

The Imam Khomeini Relief Committee (IKRC) was established on March 5, 1979.[53] Its declared goal is to support the "destitute and oppressed" and to enable them to be self-reliant. Although the committee receives a remarkable share of the annual government budget, it also runs separate commerce and financial enterprises, obtaining significant profits.

Despite its declared aim of helping the destitute, numerous reports, including those published in the regime's own media outlets, confirm that the *Emdad* Committee is part of the regime's apparatus of exporting terrorism and fundamentalism. Its website declares it has offices in Iraq, Lebanon, Azerbaijan, Syria, Tajikistan, Afghanistan and the African country of Comoros. According to state-run media, "Based on official figures, the *Emdad* Committee has official representation in 6 countries. Per its former chairman, the committee has formed popular cells in 30 countries around the world. As of 2014, the committee helps a total of 34,219 people in Lebanon, Syria, Afghanistan, Tajikistan, Iraq and Comoros. Afghanistan has the most beneficiaries with 13,200 people in need of help. Iraq is second, with 12,700 people."[54]

Some of these so-called beneficiaries are the same people who, after undergoing a series of training sessions, are sent to Syria by the Qods Force to fight for the Assad dictatorship. Many other reports describe the *Emdad* Committee's activities associated with exporting fundamentalism in various countries of the region. On July 8, 2016, Tajikistan's Ministry of Justice asked a court in the country to ban the activities of the *Emdad* Committee.[55]

---

[53] http://www.emdad.ir/

[54] 55Online.ir website, April 22, 2015

[55] Asia-Plus, July 8, 2016; http://news.tj/en/news/iran-charity-s-branch-violates-tajikistan-s-legislation-says-tajik-justice-minister

A 2016 report obtained from inside the Iranian regime indicates that the *Emdad* Committee pays monthly stipends to over 5,000 households of the Syrian dictatorship's forces killed in recent years.

On August 3, 2010, the U.S. Treasury Department designated The Imam Khomeini Relief Committee Lebanon Branch pursuant to Executive Order (E.O.) 13224.[56] Treasury stated, "Iran has provided millions of dollars to the Hezbollah-run branch in Lebanon since 2007. The IKRC has helped fund and operate Hezbollah youth training camps, which have been used to recruit future Hezbollah members and operatives. Hezbollah Secretary General Hassan Nasrallah has acknowledged the IKRC branch in Lebanon as one of Hezbollah's openly-functioning institutions linked to and funded by Iran."

On December 20, 2015, Iranian media reported that Parviz Fattah, the head of *Emdad*, had paid a visit to the Beqaa (Bekaa) Valley in south Lebanon, which is the stronghold of Hezbollah, to meet with persons who had received the committee's aide.[57]

Some of the holding companies and institutions controlled by the *Emdad* Committee are:[58]

CONSTRUCTION AND BUILDING

- Gostar Basir Construction Company
- Tehran Gostar Basir Construction Company
- Emdad Construction Expansion Development
- Nassim Construction Expansion Development

AGRICULTURE AND FOOD INDUSTRY

- Bahar Rafsanjan Agro Industrial
- Sabzdasht Fars Agricultural Company

---

[56] Fact Sheet: U.S. Treasury Department Targets Iran's Support for Terrorism Treasury Announces New Sanctions Against Iran's Islamic Revolutionary Guard Corps-Qods Force Leadership, August 3, 2010; https://www.treasury.gov/press-center/press-releases/Pages/tg810.aspx

[57] *Bazdide Raeese Komiteh Emdade Emam Khomeini as Mantaghehe Boghae Lobnan*, 20 December 2015 http://tnews.ir/news/18D854175482.html

[58] http://www.emdadimam.ir/

- Fath and Nasr Kerman Agro Industrial
- Esfahan Agriculture and Livestock Company
- Zarrin Khusheh Arak Agro Industrial
- Rezvan Emdad Golestan Agro Industrial
- Bazouy-e Keshavarz Kermanshah Agro Industrial
- Emdad Sabz Hegmataneh Agro Industrial
- Misaq Emdad Ago Industrial
- Baharan Behesht Alborz Agro Industrial
- Nar-e Mehriz Yazd Agro Industrial
- Emdad Sepahan Goldasht Agro Industrial

MINES AND MINING INDUSTRY

- Qom Mining Cooperative
- Emdad Faravar Mines
- Emdad Mines Development and Equipment
- Emdad Electricity and Energy Development
- Mines and Mining Industries Development of Kurdistan

COMMERCE

- Emdad Industry Builders
- Paydar Emdad Commerce and Investment Development

FINANCIAL

- 1,200 charity boxes

REAL ESTATE: The lands confiscated by the *Emdad* Committee in various provinces include:

- 1,349 hectares of land and farms in Fars province
- 38 hectares in Khuzestan province
- 155 hectares in Gilan province
- 158 hectares in Golestan province

- 275 hectares in Mazandaran province
- 39 hectares Hormozgan province
- 2,145 hectares in Kerman province
- 105 hectares in Yazd province
- 139 hectares in Markazi province

The committee also owns significant land and farms in other provinces, including Tehran, Esfahan, Hamedan, Semnan Alborz, Khorasan, Qazvin, Ilam, Kermanshah, Azarbaijan, Lorestan, Charmahal Bakhtiari, and Ardebil. However, there are no official reports in this regard.

6. IRGC COOPERATIVE FOUNDATION

The Islamic Revolutionary Guard Corps Cooperative Foundation (*Bonyad Taavon Sepah*) is regarded as the most powerful financial institution in the country. Article 4 of the charter of this so-called "foundation" states, "The initial investment in the foundation at the time of its founding was ten million Rials (roughly $315), contributed by the Supreme Leader."[59] Article 23 says, "All of the funds and assets of the foundation belong to His Excellency the Supreme Leader. In case of its dissolution, after settling all debts, all of the properties and assets will be handed over to His Excellency."[60]

The U.S. Treasury Department announced in December 2010 that pursuant to Executive Order (E.O.) 13382 – an authority aimed at freezing the assets of proliferators of weapons of mass destruction – *Bonyad Taavon Sepah* had been designated for providing services to the IRGC.[61]

The foundation is one of the five largest economic powerhouses in the country. Some of the commercial companies and groups of this foundation are:

A. BAHMAN AUTOMOBILE MANUFACTURING GROUP:

A considerable portion of this automotive group belongs to the IRGC Cooperative. The Ghadir Investment Company also owns a significant portion. The automobile manufacturing group itself owns the following companies:

---

[59] *Asasnameh Bonyad-e Tavon-e Sepah Pasdaran* (Statute of the IRGC Cooperative Foundation), in Farsi, <http://www.vekalatonline.ir/laws/9758/>

[60] Ibid.

[61] Fact Sheet: Treasury Designates Iranian Entities Tied to the IRGC and IRISL, December 21, 2010; https://www.treasury.gov/press-center/press-releases/Pages/tg1010.aspx

SAIPA COMPANY: Saipa is the second-largest automaker in Iran. Despite only holding 17 percent of shares in the company, in effect the IRGC is the main decision-maker and beneficiary of its profits. Saipa owns other companies, including:

- Pars Khodro (auto maker)
- Saipa Diesel
- Iran Kaveh (diesel)
- Saipa Azin
- Saipa Glass
- Iran Radiator
- Saipa Press
- Saipa Pistons
- Pouya Industries
- Niroosaz Arak
- Rayan Saipa Leasing
- Mellat Insurance
- Sayan Insurance Services
- Rayan Saipa Insurance Services
- Saipa Employee Investments
- Rana Investments
- Saipa Investments
- Rasa Capital development
- Saipa Transportation
- Saipa Parts Engineering Consulting
- Industrial Export Development Company
- Saipa Tour
- Pasargad Construction
- Saipa Sports and Culture Company

NATIONAL IRANIAN INVESTMENT COMPANY

BAHMAN INVESTMENT COMPANY

BAHMAN LEASING COMPANY

BAHMAN DIESEL (MONTAGE OF JAPANESE ISUZU TRUCKS)

IRAN CREDIT (79 PERCENT SHARE)

BAHMAN BROKERAGE

ETEMAD DEVELOPMENT INVESTMENTS

B. FINANCIAL AND CREDIT INSTITUTIONS
THAMEN INSTITUTION

THAMEN AL-A'MEH FINANCIAL AND CREDIT INSTITUTION: Also known as a credit cooperative, it has 500 branches. By early 2010, the company had lent over $13B to applicants.

C. INVESTMENT COMPANIES

BEHSHAHR INDUSTRIAL INVESTMENTS (16 PERCENT)

IRANIAN NEGIN KHATAM INVESTMENTS (OWNS SHARES IN ANSAR BANK)

SAMAN MAJD INVESTMENTS (BELONGS TO THAMEN CREDIT)

AYAK INVESTMENTS

D. ANSAR BANK:

Ansar Bank has 600 branches across Iran and is the fourth-largest bank in the country. It has formed several other companies, including:

ATLAS IRANIANS INVESTMENT HOLDING COMPANY, which is active in real estate services, and owns the following:

- Andisheh Shiva Atlas Engineering Consultants
- Atlas Pars Star
- Ferdows Iranian Garden
- Arman-e Tous Star

- Pars Planning Construction and Development (33 percent ownership)
- Eighth Tous Banagostaran (30 percent share)
- Pardis Atlas Pars (50 percent ownership)
- Atlas Iranian Construction
- Tous Gostar Investment and Urban Development
- Baghmisheh Urban Development and Residential Building
- Pardis Atlas Pars
- Iran Atlas Kish Commercial and Industry

ANSAR ELECTRONICS

HOUSHMAND IRANIAN ELECTRONICS

NOVIN PADIDEH ANSAR

ANSAR BANK EMPLOYEES COMPANY

PARS DANAYAN INVESTMENTS

IRANIAN ATLAS INVESTMENT

HAFIZ TECHNOLOGY

ANSAR CURRENCY EXCHANGE

E. INDUSTRY

KERMAN PETROCHEMICALS (25 PERCENT SHARE)

KERMANSHAH PETROCHEMICAL INDUSTRIES

ZAGROS STEEL

SHAHAB SANG MINING INDUSTRIES

IRAN WELDING INDUSTRIES

IRAN CHASSIS PRODUCTION

MOJ NASR GOSTAR TELECOMMUNICATIONS AND ELECTRONICS

EFAHAN ZINC SMELTER COMPANY

SABERIN OFOGH DEVELOPMENT ENGINEERING

ARZESH AFARINAN INDUSTRIES

BAHARIZAD WOOL WEAVING

BEHINEHSAZ AMADEH ENGINEERING

IRAN ATLAS KISH COMMERCIAL AND INDUSTRY

SINA PHARMACEUTICAL (OVER 30 PERCENT OWNERSHIP BELONGS TO IRANIAN INVESTMENTS)

F. TELECOMMUNICATIONS

MOBIN IRAN ELECTRONICS INDUSTRIES: The company's shareholders include the *Mostazafan* Foundation, Sina Investments, Kowsar Bahman Investments, Iran Electronic Equipment, and SAIRAN.

TALIA COMPANY (mobile phone operators): A portion of its shares was purchased in 2012.

MOJ NASR GOSTAR Telecommunications and Electronics

ETEMAD MOBIN CONSORTIUM: The consortium purchased 51 percent of Iran's telecommunications company and is itself comprised of three separate companies: Mobin Iran Electronics Industries; Shahriar Mahestan, which belongs to the IRGC Cooperative; and Etemad Development Investments, which belongs to *Setad*.

SAYYAR COMMUNICATIONS (provides services for Mobile Telecommunication Company of Iran, or *Hamrahe Aval*): A portion of this company's shares belongs to *Setad*. The company's largest shareholders are Iran's telecommunications company, Shahriar Mahestan, Mobin Mehr Economy, Mobin Electronics Development and the Mobin Comprehensive Communications Development. According to Massoud Mehrdadi, one of the main managers of the IRGC's commercial and financial affairs, the revenues of this company in 2012 from sales of SIM cards and phone chargers topped $2.5B.

IRAN CELL (phone operator): The company's shareholders are South Africa's MTN (49 percent share) and the Iran Electronics Industries (51 percent share).

PRODUCE AND AGRICULTURE

SHADAB KHORASAN INDUSTRIES

MAEDEH FOOD INDUSTRIES

SHADAB KHORASAN AGRO INDUSTRIES

CHARMAHAL BAKHTIARI LEAVEN FOOD

CONSTRUCTION

PREFABRICATED LIGHT STRUCTURES ENGINEERING COMPANY

JIHAD RESIDENTIAL BUILDERS (OPERATES IN 20 PROVINCES)

SEPAHAN RESIDENTIAL COMPLEX BUILDERS

RAZMANDEH RESIDENTIAL COMPLEX BUILDERS

COMMERCE AND SERVICES

PARS AIR

OIL CONTRACTORS (SOUTH PARS OIL FIELD)

RAHIAN KOMEYL COMMERCE SERVICES AND CONSULTING

PARS AIR TRAVEL

BAHRESTAN KISH COMPANY

THAMEN AL-A'MEH SERVICES CULTURAL INSTITUTION

KABOUD KAVIR ALALEH

MOHIT CONSTRUCTION

BAHARAN COMPANY

NAVID BAHMAN

KOWSARAN INSTITUTION

MISAQ BASIRAT INSTITUTION

ASR-E BAHMAN COMPANY

NEGAR NASR COMPANY

ANSAR EMPLOYEES COOPERATIVE

• PASARGAD FINANCIAL GROUP:

The Pasargad Financial Group is comprised of Pasargad Bank and several other companies, which operate in the areas of information technology, communications, electronic payment services, insurance, reinsurance, brokerages, heavy equipment leasing, commercial building leasing, construction, mining and industry, energy and other services.

Pasargad Bank is tied to the IRGC. The Pars Arian Investment Company is its largest shareholder. Among its other large shareholders are: Saipa Investments, Ghadir Investments, and Steel Industries Pension Fund.

In view of strict restrictions on IRGC-affiliated banks preceding the *velayat-e faqih*'s retreat from the nuclear program, Pasargad Bank executives made serious attempts to deny their affiliation with the IRGC. However, there is considerable evidence that the bank plays a major role in the IRGC's economic empire.

One of the large shareholders of the group is the Saman Majd Investment Company, which is affiliated with the *Thamen al-A'ameh* Credit and Financial Institution, and is part of the IRGC Cooperative Foundation. In June 2016, a scandal broke out in state-run papers showing that a banking network exists in all the mullahs' prisons, which confiscates the cash assets of the detainees. The network is part of Pasargad Bank.[62] On June 14, 2016, Pasargad denied taking advantage of prisoners in a statement. However, it admitted having branches in all prisons, saying: "In line with meeting our social responsibilities, we have been charged with this great responsibility, and despite the significant investments made in all the country's detention centers, the bank has never tried to gain profits in this area."[63]

In addition to Pasargad Bank, the group's other ventures include:

- Middle East Mining and Mining Industries Holding
- Pasargad Arian Information and Communications (FNAB)
- Pasargad Insurance
- Iranian Reinsurance Company
- Pasargad Heavy Machinery and Equipment Leasing Company
- Pasargad Leasing
- Parsargad Arzesh Afarinan Company
- Middle East Foundational Company
- Pasargad Energy Development
- Pasargad Bank Electronic Payments
- Pasargad Currency Exchange and Services
- Pasargad Bank Brokerage Services
- Eighth Urban Development and Construction Company
- Pasargad Mass Production
- Pasargad Human Capital Research and Development Institution
- Arian Investments (AICO)
- Arian Engineering and Construction Management
- Arian Pasargad Construction Management
- Pars Arian Investments
- Pasargad Bank Financial and Investment Services

---

[62] "24 hours in detention at the Great Tehran prison," state-run Qanun (law) newspaper, June 12, 2016

[63] "Response to Pasargad Bank," Asr-e Bank website, June 14, 2016

- Pasargad Bank Investments
- Arian Construction (Modabberan)
- Iran Credit Ranking Consulting
- Arian Saman Construction
- Pasargad Arian Logistics Services
- Pasargad Financial Group Pension
- Pasargad Commerce Development
- Pasargad Tadbirgaran Company
- Pasargad Future Commerce Management
- Pasargad Group International Commerce Development and Expansion
- Mana Iranian Renewal and Expansion Industries
- Zarand Iranian Steel Company
- Middle East Aftab Derakhshan (Shining Sun) Commerce
- Iranian Sirjan Steel Company
- Middle East Meyar Industrial Engineering Company
- Pars Hafez Investments

7. KHATAM AL-ANBIYA CONSTRUCTION HEADQUARTERS

The Khatam al-Anbiya Construction Headquarters is part of the IRGC. It began as a contractor of industrial and construction projects in 1989. In its charter, the most important goal of the complex is to "efficiently utilize the available construction and economic resources, capacities and talents of the IRGC to continue the Islamic Revolution."

Khatam is the largest contractor for government projects. It has 5,000 subcontractors[64] and about 135,000 employees. The cartel enjoys the complete support of the regime and has easy access to banking and financial resources and sustained contracts with no competitive bidding. It has created an operation whereby it totally dominates industrial and construction projects, as well as a portion of oil and gas deals, rendering the private sector unable to compete.

The Khatam Headquarters contracting services acts as a huge intermediary between the government and small engineering and technical companies, which have a major portion of their revenues seized by Khatam. Ownership of many of these companies occurred unilaterally or through intimidation and at times force. On July 1, 2006, Khatam took ownership of Oriental Kish Oil, which had drilling operations in some oil and gas fields of the Persian Gulf. The transfer of ownership included all projects, operations and equipment and assets, worth over $90M. Khatam resolved a commercial dispute with the Romanian-owned Grup Servicii Petroliere by firing on

---

[64] Brig. Gen. Abdollah Abdollahi, state-run Sharq newspaper, December 17, 2014

THE NEW ECONOMIC STRUCTURE: A MIND-BOGGLING CONGLOMERATE OF 14 POWERHOUSES

Romanian workers from both military helicopters and ships before boarding the (offshore) Romanian rig and holding its crew hostage, according to reports.[65]

Khatam's projects have inflicted catastrophic damage to Iran's economy and environment. Increased salt levels in the Karun River, the largest river in Iran, in addition to a portion of Iran's water crisis in recent years, are a result of the unbridled and unnecessary dam construction by Khatam.

Khatam also has extensive operations in the sectors of oil and gas and petrochemicals. For instance, it is responsible for the Phase 15 and 16 development of the South Pars oil and gas field.

State-run news agency IRNA quoted the director of the National Iranian Oil Company as saying that the Khatam Headquarters' oil contracts had surpassed $25B.[66]

Khatam-affiliated companies include:

- Tehran Gostar Company

- Oriental Oil

- Sepanir Oil and Gas Engineering (member of the board of Ansar Bank)

- Sepasad Engineering (involved in dam construction and infrastructure development projects)

- *Nour* (Light) Institution (involved in confiscation and sale of land)

- Sama Institution (involved in land and real estate sales)

- Imensazan Consultant Engineering Institute (tunnel construction and passive defense)

- Makin Institute (naval and sea structures)

- Rahab Institute (tunnel construction and drilling)

- Fater Engineering Institute (tunnel construction)

- Sahel Construction (railroads)

---

[65] http://www.voanews.com/a/a-13-2006-08-22-voa26/323128.html

[66] State-run News Agency, IRNA, July 30, 2011.

IRAN: THE RISE OF THE REVOLUTIONARY GUARDS' FINANCIAL EMPIRE

In October 2007, The United States Treasury Department designated Khatam al-Anbiya under Executive Order (E.O.) 13382, which freezes the assets of designated proliferators of weapons of mass destruction and their supporters.[67] Other Khatam affiliated companies — Oriental Oil, Sahel Construction, and Sepasad Engineering — were covered by the same designation. In February 2010, Treasury took a further step and designated under the same order IRGC General Rostam Qasemi, the commander of Khatam al-Anbiya Construction Headquarters, as well as four subsidiary companies, Fater Engineering Institute, Imensazen Consultant Engineers Institute (ICEI), Makin Institute, and Rahab Institute.[68]

---

[67] Fact Sheet: Designation of Iranian Entities and Individuals for Proliferation Activities and Support for Terrorism, October 25, 2007; https://www.treasury.gov/press-center/press-releases/Pages/hp644.aspx

[68] Treasury Targets Iran's Islamic Revolutionary Guard Corps, February 10, 2010; https://www.state.gov/r/pa/prs/ps/2010/02/136595.htm

8. BASSIJ COOPERATIVE FOUNDATION

The *Bassij* Cooperative Foundation belongs to the paramilitary *Bassij* Force, considered one of the five forces of the IRGC. The foundation has a large number of holdings and financial institutions, including:

• IRANIAN MEHR ECONOMIC INVESTMENTS

This company has an extensive presence in the Tehran Stock Exchange. Much like other economic powerhouses affiliated with the Supreme Leader's office, the company's star rose overnight. Former director of the company Abbas Rezai said in 2009: "We took over the Iranian Mehr Economic Investment Company 32 months ago with $6.3M to $9.4M. I am now leaving a company that has $4.4B worth of investments."[69]

The affiliates of this company include:

• ZINC MINING DEVELOPMENT HOLDING COMPANY

- Kalsimin Company
- Bandar Abbas Zinc Production
- Acid Producers of Zanjan and Alvand Zinc Workers
- Iran National Lead and Zinc Company
- Bafeq Zinc Smelting

IRAN MINING RESOURCE EXTRACTION

IRAN ZINC PRODUCTION

---

[69] Donyay-e Eqtesad (World of Economics), January 20, 2010

PARSIAN CHEMICAL CATALYST

ZANGAN ZINC INDUSTRIAL

ANGOURAN MINERS

ZINC DEVELOPMENT AND COMMERCE

MEHVARAN ANDISHEH INVESTMENT

NON-FERROUS METALS ENGINEERING AND RESEARCH

POUYA ALPHA MACHINERY

SHAHROUD NORTHEASTERN MINING AND INDUSTRY

JAM OMID ALBORZ

• IRANIAN TAJALI MEHR COMPANY:

A construction holding company, it is comprised of the following companies:

- Sharq Farasoo Company
- Ansar Construction
- Kousha Paydar Engineering Consulting
- Kowsar Azarbaijan Company
- Eftekhar Khuzestan Company
- Techno-Kar Company (produces fuel distribution pumps and fuel tanks)

• IRAN TRACTOR MANUFACTURING (TABRIZ):

Comprised of the following companies:

- Engine Manufacturers
- Azarbaijan Diesel Car Manufacturers
- Kurdistan Tractor Manufacturing
- Oroumieh Tractor Manufacturing
- Ougiran Tractor Manufacturing

- Iran Casting and Tractor Manufacturing Company

- Tractor Industrial Services

- Tractor Industrial Machinery

- Tractor Casting

- Tractor Engine Makers

- Tractor Blacksmithing

- Tractor Parts and Engineering

- Tractor Machinery and Equipment Makers

- Siba Engine

- Tajiran

- Motira

PARSIAN BANK

IRAN ALUMINUM INDUSTRIES (IRAL CO)

ESFAHAN MOBARAKEH STEEL COMPANY: A portion of the industry is owned by the IRGC Cooperative Foundation, while another portion is owned by the Social Welfare Investment Company.

MIDDLE EAST TIDE WATER COMPANY: The company operates in Bandar Abbas's Rajai port, where up to 60 percent of Iran's imports and exports are conducted.

IRAN MEHR-E EQTESAD BANK: The bank was formerly called the Mehr Financial and Credit Institution (charity fund for former Bassij members). According to the bank's website, it started its operations with a $300 investment "gifted by His Excellency the Supreme Leader." The gift was increased in several stages up to $125 million.[70] The bank represents the largest unofficial banking network, with 700 branches and 8 million depositors around the country.

INDUSTRIAL DEVELOPMENT INVESTMENTS COMPANY

AZARBAIJAN DEVELOPMENT INVESTMENTS COMPANY

---

[70] goo.gl/lDwbVt

MEHR RESIDENTIAL AND CONSTRUCTION INVESTMENT COMPANY

ANGOURAN MINE DEVELOPMENT

TOUS GOSTAR COMPANY

SADID PIPES AND EQUIPMENT COMPANY

JABER IBN HAYAN PHARMACEUTICALS

TABRIZ TRACTOR MANUFACTURING SOCCER CLUB

IRANIAN MEHR-E EQTESAD BROKERAGE

KOUSHA PAYDAR COMPANY

KOWSAR AZARBAIJAN COMPANY

MEHR FARSIGHTED COMMERCE SERVICES

ATIEH TADBIRGARAN COMPANY

9. GHADIR INVESTMENT COMPANY

Ghadir is one of the most important investment companies in Iran.[71] Although tied to the Defense Department, government institutions do not have authority or influence over it; the Supreme Leader controls it. The company controls over 16 percent of cement production in Iran, and 5.2 percent of cement production in the Middle East and North Africa, which translates into 0.4 percent of total cement production in the world.

In the United States, Ghadir Investment Company, has been sanctioned under Iranian Transactions and Sanctions Regulations by the U.S. Treasury Department, which requires U.S. persons to block the property and interests in property of this entity.[72]

Some of the companies operating under Ghadir are:

• THE PARSIAN OIL AND GAS DEVELOPMENT GROUP,
whose subsidiaries include:

- Tabriz Oil Refinery
- Shiraz Oil Refinery
- Pardis Petrochemicals (the largest urea fertilizer producer in the Middle East)
- Zagros Petrochemicals (the world's largest producer of methanol)
- Kermanshah Petrochemicals

---

[71] http://www.ghadir-group.com/Modules/CMS/CMSPages/ShowPage.aspx?MItemID=vUUvvMcxvMbU

[72] https://sanctionssearch.ofac.treas.gov/Details.aspx?id=5814

- Shiraz Petrochemicals
- Tabriz Petrochemicals
- Khorasan Petrochemicals
- Kian Petrochemicals
- Pars Petrochemicals
- Hamoun Sepahan Investments
- International Petrochemicals Commerce Company
- Nirou Rail Transport Company

• INTERNATIONAL CONSTRUCTION DEVELOPMENT COMPANY, whose subsidiaries includes:

- ASP
- Baghmisheh Residential Builders
- Royay-e Zendegi Kish
- Ghadir Engineering Consulting
- Pars Structures Engineering and Construction
- Tisa Kish Company
- Fars Shelter
- Ghadir Khuzestan
- Azarbaijan Construction
- Paya Ofogh Structures
- Narenjestan Gostar Company
- Behestan Pars Company

• GHADIR CAPITAL AND INDUSTRY DEVELOPMENT COMPANY, whose subsidiaries include:

- Sharq Cement
- Sepahan Cement
- Kurdistan Cement
- Dashtestan Cement

- Dey Investments
- Azar Investments
- Sarouj Boushehr Cement
- Ghadir Mehr Iranian Engineering Research

• GHADIR INTERNATIONAL MINING AND INDUSTRIAL DEVELOPMENT COMPANY:

Through this holding company, Ghadir Investments has purchased iron ore mines; the Zarshouran mine, which is the largest gold mine in Iran located in West Azarbaijan; a titanium mine in Kerman's Kahnouj; and a zinc mine in Semnan province's Mehdi Abad. Some of the largest companies in the conglomerate are:

- Alloy Steel Company
- Sang Ahan Iron Ore
- Iranian Iron and Steel
- South Aluminum Industries Complex
- Pars Industries International Development
- Motogen
- Shahid Qazi Pharmaceuticals
- Shahid Bahonar Wood

• GHADIR INDUSTRIAL AND COMMERCE COMPANY
(financial and commercial holdings), whose subsidiaries include:

- Ghadir Caspian Steel Company
- Ghadir Management and Commercial Services
- Peyman Permanent Commerce
- Sepehr Pars Deposits
- Etezad Ghadir Investments
- Sepehr Iranian Insurance Services
- Arman Resource Provisions Management

- Effective Management Company (*kar'amad*)
- Zarrin Persia Investments
- Jebel Ali Masader
- Saderat Bank Brokerage
- Rahbar Informatics Services
- Alvand Ghadir Development Investments

• GHADIR POWER AND ENERGY INVESTMENTS,
whose subsidiaries include:

- Gilan Masir Electricity
- Gilan Power Generation Management (*Towlid-e Barq-e Gilan*)
- Ghadir Oxin Energy Development
- MAPNA[73] Khuzestan Power Generation
- Ghadir Energy Hamoun Abu Mousa
- Lamerd Power Generation

• KISH NEGIN INTERNATIONAL ONSHORE AND OFFSHORE DEVELOPMENT
(Ghadir's marine transport holding), whose subsidiaries include:

- Iran Marine Shipping Services
- Kish South Iran Dariaban
- Ghadir Sepehr Transportation

---

[73] Stands for the Farsi abbreviation of the company name: *Modiriat-e Porojehay-e Nirougahi-e Iran* (MAPNA) – Management of Power Generation Projects in Iran.

10. ARMED FORCES SOCIAL WELFARE INVESTMENT ORGANIZATION (SATA)

The Armed Forces Social Welfare Investment Organization (SATA) is made up of a wide range of industrial and investment companies, including:

• ARMED FORCES INVESTMENTS COMPANY, WHICH INCLUDES:

▶ Maroun Petrochemicals Complex

▶ Pars Petrochemicals Complex

▶ North Drilling Company (Setad also owns shares in this company)

▶ Boushehr Petrochemicals Complex

▶ Gilan Combined Cycle Power Generation (*Sikl-e Tarkibi*)

▶ Gilan Production Management (*Modiriat-e Bahr-e Bardari*)

11. KHATAM AL-OSIA HEADQUARTERS

Khatam al-Osia is tied to the Department of Defense and was founded on the orders of Khamenei in 2010. It is a consortium comprised of five large oil and gas contractors. Khatam al-Osia is in essence a cartel of contractors, formed by a large number of contracting companies who leverage political influence to win government contracts without going through a formal process (i.e. without competitive bids).[74] They then subcontract to engineering companies, winning large sums of profits at the other end.

The complex carries out construction and oil projects. It replaced Shell and Repsol in developments in the South Pars field.

Below are some of the most significant oil and gas contracts awarded to Khatam al-Osia in recent years:

- Development of South Pars 15 and 16 phases, worth about $2B
- Development of South Pars common fields, phases 22 to 24, worth about $5B to $6B
- Development of the third section of the sixth cross-country gas pipeline, worth about $1.3B
- Development of the first phase of the seventh cross-country gas pipeline (so-called "Peace Pipeline"), worth about $1.3B
- Development of gas refinery in Ilam, worth roughly $120M
- Neka-Jask oil pipeline, worth over $3B
- Construction of three oil pipelines in Khorasan, Kerman and Hormozgan provinces, worth about $850M
- Development of Halgan and Baghoun gas fields, worth about $1B

---

[74] Majid Rezvani, deputy director at the Khatam al-Osia: "The contracts are awarded to us without going through the formal process," state-run Fars news agency, February 5, 2013.

- Production of Liquid National Gas, worth about $500M
- Construction of methane, ethylene and LNG pipelines, worth in total over $1B
- Tehran-Mashhad railway electrification project
- Construction of the Ramsar beach ring road

Khatam al-Osia has also taken over the assets of two banks, which include:

- Arak Pars Wagon
- Engineering and Urban Development Holding
- Rail Holding
- Parsian Engineering Equipment Company

12. STATE SECURITY FORCES (NAJA) COOPERATIVE FOUNDATION

The foundation is tied to the Iranian regime's State Security Forces (SSF or its Farsi abbreviation NAJA). However, the Interior Ministry has no supervision over it. Its cooperative foundation, which today is one of the largest holding companies in Iran, was established in 1997, but grew to a remarkable scale after 2005. In 2014, state-run media estimated the assets of this foundation to be over $3.2B.[75]

The enterprises of this foundation include:

QAVAMIN BANK, which owns:

- Amin Naqsh Pardazan Construction
- Sayan Card
- Ofogh Qarn Development
- Yas Cultural, Education, and Sports Institute
- Mehregan Economic Group

MEHREGAN INVESTMENTS (which owns shares in Sang Ahan Iron Ore Mining and Aloumorad)

NAJA HOPE INSURANCE FUND (*Bimeh Omid*)

---

[75] Payesh Press, September 24, 2014.

NAJA SCIENCE, EDUCATION AND RECREATION INSTITUTE

NAJA CONSUMER GOODS INSTITUTE

RESIDENTIAL COOPERATIVE AND INVESTMENT FUND

SAVING THE ARTS INSTITUTE (NAJI-E HONAR), a film production company

RAHGOSHA INSTITUTE (traffic police contractor)

PAYDAR-E QARN BUILDING AND CONSTRUCTION (owns 51 companies, including Nirou Engineering and Construction, Amin Naji Sazan, Tehran Gostar Wire, Takestan Wire and Steel, Sabz Andishan Mass Producers, Paydar Faza Kar Qarn Building and Construction)

TAVAN POUYA CAPITAL, a trade and commerce holding (includes Najm and Chit Rey Stores, Naji Pars Co, and Shafaq Tavan Co)

INDUSTRY AND MINING HOLDING COMPANY (includes Naji Nashr (Rah-e Farda), Naji Poushesh, Zagros Noush Mehregan, Arsh-e Natanz Cement, Asia Cotton Weaving, and Kish Bio-Implant)

SERVICES HOLDING COMPANY

TRANSPORTATION HOLDING COMPANY

CAR IMPORTS CO.

PARDIS HOTELS GROUP, which owns Thamen al-Hojaj hotels, Bakhtar, Sadr, Negin, Zomorrod, Parsa (in Mashhad), Boustan, Baghcheh, Bagh-e Pardis (in Tehran), Molla Sadra (Shiraz), Narges Ziba Kenar (in Rasht), Khezerabad Complex in Sari, and Abadan Karvansara Hotel

MEGA MALL, HYPER ME, AND YAS SUPERMARKETS

NAJI RESEARCH AND DEVELOPMENT COMPANY (includes Laleh Computers)

OFOQ PERSIAN GULF ENERGY DEVELOPMENT

MOSQUE DEVELOPMENT OFFICE

NAJI QADR COMPANY (includes Marine Structures Engineering and Development Company)

NAJI TRAVEL (includes the Tuka Tour and Gharb Asia Tours travel agencies)

PARS HOTEL INVESTMENTS COMPANY

ATR-E GOL-E YAS PRODUCERS AND DISTRIBUTERS COOPERATIVE (has 10 companies, including Yas Law Office)

13. ARMY COOPERATIVE FOUNDATION (BTAJA)

The foundation's economic enterprises include:

ARMED FORCES CREDIT UNION

COOPERATIVE AND INVESTMENT FUND OF THE ARMY

RESIDENTIAL BUILDERS OF THE ARMY COOPERATIVE FOUNDATION

INSURANCE FUND OF THE ARMY COOPERATIVE FOUNDATION

SABA INSURANCE FOUNDATION

INVESTMENTS AND DEVELOPMENT FUND

QAEM CONSTRUCTION HEADQUARTER

ESPADANA INDUSTRY GROUP OF FACTORIES (ESFAHAN)

UPVC ALUMINUM DOORS AND WINDOWS

DOUBLE-PANE WINDOW MANUFACTURERS

WOODEN DOORS MANUFACTURERS

ALUMINUM FAÇADE (COMPOSITE) MANUFACTURERS

AZAD EDUCATION INSTITUTE

14. JOINT CHIEFS OF THE ARMED FORCES COOPERATIVE FOUNDATION (VDJA)

The foundation owns multiple companies. According to its former president, "The resources of the VDJA Cooperative have increased from $31.5M in 2009 to $2.2B in 2013. Its budget has also increased from $20.5M in 2009 to $470M in 2013."[76]

---

[76] Ahmad Vahidi, former Minister of Defense, quoted by Javan Press Club, August 18, 2013.

DEALING WITH IRAN: INTERNAL KNOTS AND EXTERNAL OBSTACLES

Since the nuclear deal, massive economic challenges, such as limits on Iran's oil exports and exclusion from international financial networks (SWIFT), have largely been removed. Many companies, especially in Europe and Asia, have sent economic delegations to Tehran to evaluate the possibility of trade. From that perspective, we expect that the more transparent environment will enable us to better understand Iran's deep-rooted economic disorder. And from that same perspective, a question arises: Why has the economic recession deepened despite the lifting of sanctions following the JCPOA? And, what explains the profound caution on the part of foreign companies – contrary to earlier expectations and voices of optimism – to deal with Iran or to invest in the country?

There is no doubt that the dramatic decline in oil prices in 2015 and the first half of 2016 put a dent in government coffers, which increased pressure on the Iranian economy as a whole. But a more careful examination reveals that there are fundamental issues at play, stemming in essence from the gridlock brought about by the policies of the Iranian regime. These problems can be summed up in two categories: domestic and external challenges.

DOMESTIC CHALLENGES

On June 7, 2016, the Iranian foreign ministry submitted an official report to the Majlis (parliament), evaluating in unprecedentedly blunt terms the results of the nuclear deal. The report stated that the most important challenge remained the lack of stability and security in Iran, adding, "The most important problem and challenge that the JCPOA faces is the absence of a climate in the country that promotes trust and reassurance for foreign parties. ... The most significant factor in these companies' cost-benefit analysis when it comes to dealing with Iran is the degree to which they trust this exchange and its immediate environment. If a company does not conclude that the destination market presents a secure atmosphere for investment, trade or essentially any form of economic cooperation, then it would certainly not invest, or transfer technology, or enter into large projects, or get involved in large trade deals. In the chaotic environment of the Middle East – gripped by the flight of capital – and in an environment characterized by doubt with respect to the commitment of all parties to comply with the JCPOA, it is natural for many companies to pause and reflect on the situation. In order to solve this problem, in conjunction with creating a sense of competition, we must promote a climate of assurance for our economic interlocutors so that fear and worry about dealing with Iran give way to an eagerness for cooperation."[77]

The dearth of security and stability, and absence of "a climate of assurance" highlighted by the foreign ministry have various political, legal and economic aspects. The following sections provide explanations of the most important relevant points.

---

[77] Matne Kamele Gozareshe Vezarate Omoure Kharejeh be Majles dar bareh ejraye BARJAM, Tasnim News Agency, April 17, 2016, available at https://www.tasnimnews.com/fa/news/1395/01/29/1051333

THE SUPREMACY OF THE SUPREME LEADER

The global consulting firm Control Risks said in a 2016 analysis that "Iran market risks will remain despite implementation of JCPOA". The analysis underscored the following: "Reputational risks will be significant for companies with business in the US and other jurisdictions in the Middle East where Iran remains a highly politicised and sensitive issue; Hidden ownership structures of Iranian companies will pose additional risks to investors from a reputational and compliance perspective; The reinstating of sanctions (so-called 'snap back') will remain a possibility throughout the implementation of the JCPOA over the next decade; Sectors of strategic importance to the government and/or with high levels of state ownership will likely be affected by regulatory unpredictability and political interference; A lack of local understanding of international compliance requirements and entrenched corrupt behaviours will challenge corporate governance standards imposed by foreign companies."[78]

With respect to the interference of government agencies, undoubtedly the most important player is the *velayat-e faqih* and its affiliates, including the IRGC, State Security Forces, Bassij, *Setad*, Oppressed Foundation, Astan-e Qods, and the Ghadir Company, among others. As discussed, these entities have taken hold of a vast portion of the Iranian economy, particularly banking and financial institutions as well as profitable factories and trade organizations. Their extensive shadow of domination, primarily intended to sustain funding for the regime's warmongering in Syria and Iraq, for the Lebanese Hezbollah and to pay for the huge costs of maintaining security inside Iran, means that in practice all foreign deals will be made with them.

Pierre Fabiani, former head of the French oil giant TOTAL's branch in Iran, now works as the deputy Iran director at an association of French oil and gas companies called GEP-AFTP. He told *Le Monde* newspaper: "My recommendation to all our member companies is that they must conduct detailed investigations to determine if their

---

[78] Control Risks, January 2016. (https://www.controlrisks.com/en/our-thinking/analysis/iran-risks-remain)

Despite Iranian regime's hopes, the nuclear deal has not fixed its economic woes

potential Iranian partners are tied to the IRGC. If yes, then they should step away from the partnership."[79]

POLITICAL STRIFE

The political infighting at the pinnacle of the regime's hierarchy, aggravated by the probability of Khamenei's death in the near term and ensuing conflict to determine his replacement, have destabilized the regime in its entirety. On two occasions in 2015, Khamenei himself articulated the imperative of selecting a replacement. The January 8, 2017 death of Ali Akbar Hashemi Rafsanjani, the head of the so-called "moderate" faction and key to the regime's internal equilibrium, removed any real prospects for political, and therefore economic stability. In the aftermath of his death, it is expected that the political weight of Hassan Rouhani will diminish, the risks inherent in dealing with Iran will increase, and the mullahs will increasingly turn to more aggressive behaviors in the region.

---

[79] Quoted in the French daily *Le Monde*, April 22, 2016.

Head of the judiciary Sadeq Larijani is a high-ranking mullah with 63 bank accounts under his name. He is a prime example of the corruption that fills the Iranian bureaucracy

At the same time, fallout from the next presidential elections, scheduled for May 2017, is already weighing on the economy. Beyond indicating a fraction of the bureaucratic corruption, the revelations about the absurd salaries of bank chiefs, heads of insurance companies and senior government officials, or the leaks about the 63 bank accounts belonging to the high-ranking mullah and the head of the Judiciary, Sadeq Larijani, are indicative of the growing disputes and divisions brewing among the regime's factions. Their intensity is reflected in the arrest of the head of Mellat Bank (the largest Iranian bank), an unusual move that was spearheaded by the IRGC, as well as the official request of the "revolutionary court" to sentence the brother of president Rouhani to life in prison. Such occurrences have removed any semblance of a "promising" environment for healthy economic activity and stability.

The political conflicts and infighting have naturally spilled over into the economic realm. For example, new government-sanctioned oil contracts have motivated clashes between the government on the one hand and the armed forces and their political affiliates on the other. The armed forces believe that the oil ministry has signed these contracts without giving due attention to national interests and the regime's sovereignty. On the other side, Bijan Namdar Zangeneh, the oil minister, claims that his opponents are worried about their own factional and financial interests.

Zangeneh began his tenure in 2013 by launching an extensive reshuffling campaign impacting the ministry's management. In a short span of time, he sacked 60 managers, replacing them with former colleagues and loyalists.

The Rouhani government's actions, especially in the oil and gas sectors and its related industries, have invited fervent opposition from the IRGC and their political allies, to the extent that some deputies in parliament are calling for the reopening of the Crescent Petroleum case in which corruption charges were made against Zangeneh. The dispute was so drawn out and taxing that Zangeneh implicitly signaled that he would voluntarily step down from his post at the end of the government's term in 2017.

As a concession to the IRGC, the government picked an IRGC veteran commander, Rostam Qassemi, a former head of the giant Khatam al-Anbiya construction cartel, as an advisor to the president's first deputy. But on February 1, 2016, the government announced its decision to fire Qassemi, whom it viewed as actively obstructing the implementation of planned oil contracts. Two days prior, a number of members of the paramilitary Bassij Force had staged a gathering in front of the oil ministry headquarters to voice support for the IRGC and protest against new oil contracts between Iran and the West.

Clearly, oil pacts had taken center stage in the factional infighting. Several months later, Rouhani's cabinet finally gave in and recognized the partnering role of the Persian oil company (an affiliate of the Barkat Foundation tied to Khamenei) and Khatam Construction with foreign companies investing in new oil projects. In another concession, in June 2016, Rouhani's government and the IRGC came to an agreement, awarding 50 construction projects to Khatam Construction.

FINANCIAL INSTABILITY

The Iranian economy is suffering from profound financial instability, the most visible manifestations of which are bankruptcies in the collapsing banking sector. This phenomenon, the most important development in Iran's political economy a year after the implementation of JCPOA, is the outcome of a trend that started at least 10 years ago. But its acceleration in recent months has

Iran's Central Bank lends absurd amounts of money to members of the regime with almost no interest

prompted official institutions to use for the first time the terms "insolvency" and "bankruptcy" to describe the situation.

The banking sector is facing a severe capital shortfall and reduction in financial quality. According to a report by the research center of the regime's parliament (Majlis), the Capital Adequacy Ratio (CAR) for most banks is only 4% in Iran, compared to a range of 12-19% in neighboring countries. Non-performing loans (NPL) account for at least 17% of the total value of loans, a significant departure from those of neighboring countries, which largely stay in the single digits. This situation diminishes the capacity of Iranian banks to finance large investments in the post-nuclear deal climate.[80]

The level of "delinquent" or "bad debt" has reached extraordinary heights. Delayed debts are those whose payments have not been received for more than six months. Delinquent loans are those which have had no payments for over 18 months. The following figures show the pace of growth in delinquent bank loans during the Rouhani period:[81]

---

[80] http://bankemardom.ir/1395/03/19/27273/

[81] The state-run daily *Ta'adol*, April 20, 2016, quoting the Central Bank.

- MARCH 2013: 67,000,000,000,000 TOMANS (USD $20,703,000,000)

- MARCH 2014: 72,600,000,000,000 TOMANS (USD $22,433,400,000)

- MARCH 2015: 91,700,000,000,000 TOMANS (USD $28,335,300,000)

In Iran, 15.4% of all loans are delinquent. By comparison, in Europe (excluding Ireland, Greece and Italy) the rate is 3.9%.

The audit secretary of the Iranian Central Bank said in December 2015 that the share of bad debt in the banking system is 64%.[82] This translates to $18.5B, and is unlikely to be paid. According to the same official, the make-up of non-performing loans are: 21% overdue, 13% delinquent, 44% bad debt. The state-affiliated website Tabnak ran the eye-opening headline in June 2016 that "most banks are effectively bankrupt."[83]

In an environment of rampant corruption, numerous factors have created this crisis:

☑ "Preferential" and political loans provided to IRGC-affiliated companies or regime officials who then refuse to pay them back;

☑ The drastic jump in the amount of government debt to banks;

☑ Banks' venturing into real estate, which has been hit hard by a dramatic recession;

☑ And, finally, the acquisition of large companies and holdings by banks, which has in turn reduced liquidity.

In this context, banks keep deposit interest rates high in order to strengthen their capital position by attracting social savings. The rate being paid by some banks is close to 30%. It is worth noting that interest rates in countries like France and the United States are currently less than 1%. In June 2016, in accordance with a directive from the Central Bank, the rate was reduced to 18%. However, given the existence of at least six thousand unofficial or illegal financial and credit institutions operating in Iran, it is unlikely that the Central Bank's directive will have much impact. Extraordinary profits have flooded the banks, depriving production and manufacturing. As a result, the banking system is on the one hand incapable of

---

[82] State-affiliated *Tabnak* website, June 7, 2016.

[83] Ibid

making loans to the manufacturing sector and on the other hand is aggravating the current recession by hoarding the money supply.

At present, the Central Bank is reportedly studying plans to spur mergers, acquisitions, liquidations and reforms in the banking sector to reduce the number of banks.[84]

PERVASIVE CORRUPTION

Another aspect of the financial instability is the profound corruption that is seemingly omnipresent in all layers of the bureaucracy. On a routine basis, competing political factions in the Iranian regime expose rivals' corruption, all ranging in the billions of dollars. Examples of the systematic corruption spreading through the Iranian economy like wildfire include:

- ☑ Import/export irregularities, including irrational tariffs, in conjunction with sudden and over-night regulations and directives;

- ☑ Astronomical bank loans to senior regime officials and IRGC-affiliated enterprises, the funds of which are then redirected towards unproductive activities with no multiplier effects;

- ☑ Tax exemptions for and tax evasion by *velayat-e faqih-*affiliated enterprises;

- ☑ Awards of contracts in violation of pertinent regulations;

- ☑ Financial transactions and deals based on secret information and intelligence not available to the public;

- ☑ Sale of shares in state-affiliated companies at unjustifiably suppressed prices to the IRGC and *bonyads* (foundations) run by the *velayat-e faqih*;

- ☑ Unregulated oil sales;

- ☑ Destructive seizures of public lands and natural resources;

- ☑ Government-run sports institutions and government insistence on running commercial sports enterprises.

---

[84] State-run *Mehr* News Agency, June 8, 2016.

LACK OF COMPETITION AND OBSTRUCTIVE REGULATIONS

Spontaneous decision-making has sowed confusion and instability in banking rules and policy, disrupting financial markets. At the same time, the instability of the management of large-scale state-run economic institutions has intensified volatility and lack of trust in the overall economy. Mohammad Lahouti, the chairman of the Confederation of Exporters, has said: "Currently, there are more than 1,600 regulations that hamper trade, which shows that we are witnessing an upsurge of disruptive legislation; rules that are at times contradictory and inconsistent with one another. ... At present, there are extreme difficulties relevant to regulation for foreign investments and even registering a company."[85]

In order to launch any official economic activity in Iran's private sector, one has to obtain a lengthy catalog of permits. According to state-run media, 23 separate government organs are required to approve permits for trade in Iran.[86] Moreover, once a production facility, for example, becomes sufficiently profitable, in addition to the various tax-collecting entities and social organizations, dozens of other institutions start claiming a share of the profits from the entrepreneur. And even if he gains special privileges and favors with the regime's officials in order to overcome these obstacles, government organs can make their presence known at any time by regulating prices – ostensibly to fight price hikes and inflation, thereby artificially limiting the entrepreneur's chances for growth.

In reality, economic activity in Iran in all spheres is dominated by the special whims and "directives" of the bureaucracy. The back-breaking control of the regime over the entire economic system and the astonishing growth of extremely disruptive and obstructive rules and regulations severely limit freedom of action, leaving little or no room for genuine free-market competition in Iran.

---

[85] State-run *Ebtekar* daily, February 27, 2016 (http://www.ebtekarnews.com/?newsid=36068) .

[86] State-run media, December 29, 2016.

RECESSION AND BANKRUPTCY

Not even a 200% increase in revenues due to oil exports has been able to jolt the moribund Iranian economy to life. Mohammad Baqer Nobakht, chairman of the Management and Planning Organization (formerly known as the Plan and Budget Organization) said in 2016 that the oil revenues for the first half of the Iranian calendar year (starting in March 2016) had been used to pay the previous year's expenses.[87] The government is facing a dramatic budget shortfall, which has translated into suspensions of the overwhelming majority of infrastructure projects.

According to Economic Minister Ali Tayyebnia, government debt to banks and private companies has quickly ballooned to somewhere between $200B to $230B.[88] By some accounts, the total value of Iran's blocked assets, unfrozen after the lifting of international sanctions, was approximately $43B. There are reports, however, that the Iranian regime has allocated the bulk of that money to revive its war machine in Syria and Iraq.[89] According to the State Department's Annual Country Reports on Terrorism 2015, "Iran has provided hundreds of millions of dollars in support of Hizballah in Lebanon and has trained thousands of its fighters at camps in Iran."[90]

There is no need for lengthy lists to document the obvious disappearance of manufacturing facilities in Iran. Factories board up and workers are laid off every day. For example, in June 2016, the governor of Borujerd province in western Iran, Moselm Pour-Ghasemian, said thousands of workers lost their jobs after 80 factories closed down in that region alone. 50,000 workers had lost their jobs,

---

[87] ISNA, December 26, 2016.

[88] ISNA, January 15, 2017.

[89] Even as early as January 21, 2016 when international sanctions were just being lifted, U.S. Secretary of State John Kerry, who led nuclear negotiations with Iran, admitted that some sanctions relief money for Iran will go to terrorism. CNN quoted him as saying, "I think that some of it will end up in the hands of the IRGC or other entities, some of which are labeled terrorists." (http://www.cnn.com/2016/01/21/politics/john-kerry-money-iran-sanctions-terrorism/)

[90] State Department's Annual Country Report On Terrorism, U.S. State Department, Chapter 3-State Sponsored Terrorism, 6/2/16 (https://www.state.gov/j/ct/rls/crt/2015/257520.htm).

creating a "livelihood crisis,"[91] he said. That crisis is so palpable that the highest official in the regime, Ali Khamenei, stated in a speech on March 20, 2016, that 60 percent of the country's productive capacity was "untapped."[92] Analysts estimate that two thirds of Iran's total industrial capacity has either vanished or remains idle.

The most significant challenges for the manufacturing sector are "insufficient access to the money supply, inadequate markets, internal company disputes, the high cost of raw materials, faulty machinery,"[93] a corrupt bureaucracy, the plethora of onerous rules and regulations, and excessive imports flooding the domestic markets with foreign-made goods.

Regime officials note that "industrial parks have become ghost towns and production facilities have been turned into storage yards as a form of revenue generation."[94] In fact, many manufacturing plants in Iran are dealing with "hidden bankruptcies."

Iran has been falling every year with respect to the World Bank's "resolving insolvency" ranking, which measures the time, cost, outcome and recovery rate for a commercial insolvency, as well as the strength of the legal framework for insolvency. According to the 2014 World Bank Ease of Doing Business report, Iran ranked 129 among 189 economies[95]. In the 2015 report, its ranking fell to 138.[96] In 2016, it fell another two spots to 140.[97] And, as of 2017, it has dropped to 156 among 190 countries.[98]

---

[91] The Media Express, June 17, 2016 (https://themediaexpress.com/2016/06/17/closure-of-80-factories-has-left-thousands-unemployed-says-iranian-government/)

[92] The text of his speech is published on Khamenei's official website: "According to the reports that I have received, today, about 60 percent of our productive capacity is untapped and unused. Some [of our industries] work less than their capacity and some do not work at all." (http://english.khamenei.ir/news/3550/Islamic-Republic-Has-Destroyed-Enemy-Trenches-Inside-Iran)

[93] Some of the reasons identified by deputy head of Iran Small Industries and Industrial Parks Organization, Farshad Moqimi, ISNA, July 31, 2015.

[94] State-run Fars News Agency, June 23, 2016.

[95] http://www.doingbusiness.org/~/media/WBG/DoingBusiness/Documents/Annual-Reports/English/DB14-Full-Report.pdf

[96] http://www.doingbusiness.org/~/media/WBG/DoingBusiness/Documents/Annual-Reports/English/DB15-Full-Report.pdf

[97] http://www.doingbusiness.org/~/media/WBG/DoingBusiness/Documents/Annual-Reports/English/DB16-Full-Report.pdf

[98] http://www.doingbusiness.org/~/media/WBG/DoingBusiness/Documents/Annual-Reports/English/DB17-Report.pdf

The Iranian economy is in dire need of foreign investment, particularly in the oil industry. According to Iranian oil ministry estimates, Iran needs more than $180B in investments in the oil and gas sector over the next decade.[99] But officials have thus far been unable to chart a clear course toward attracting such funds. In January 2017, a year after the international sanctions were lifted, Italian energy giant ENI's CEO Claudio Descalzi signaled pessimism about Tehran's ability to pull in this level of capital. "In today's market, finding $150 to $200 billion to invest in Iran is not something that can be done in a second" especially at a time when oil companies are cutting costs,[100] he said, adding that companies like Shell, British Petroleum, TOTAL or Eni do not have a real interest in accelerating investments in countries where political risks remain high.

---

[99] "Iranian officials … (estimate that) the key oil and gas sectors need about $180 billion of funds for expansion and maintenance during the next decade." Reuters, January 15, 2017. (http://uk.reuters.com/article/iran-economy-plan-idUKL5N1F408K)/

[100] Reuters, January 17, 2017 (http://uk.reuters.com/article/uk-eni-iran-idUKKCN0UV0NM).

FOREIGN OBSTACLES

The regime's Supreme Leader Ali Khamenei said in a speech on March 20, 2016: "Notice that today, in all western countries and in all those countries that are under their influence, our banking transactions have been blocked. We have a problem bringing our wealth – which has been kept in their banks – back to the country. We have a problem conducting various financial transactions, which require the assistance of banks. And when we pursue the matter ... it becomes clear that they are afraid of the Americans. ... This is what we are witnessing in front of our eyes! This means a complete loss!"[101]

For his part, former U.S. President Barack Obama said during a press conference in Washington on April 1, 2016: "When [Iranian officials] launched ballistic missiles with slogans calling for the destruction of Israel, that makes businesses nervous. There is some geopolitical risk that is heightened when they see that taking place. If Iran continues to ship missiles to Hezbollah, that gets businesses nervous. ... But Iran has to understand what every country in the world understands, which is businesses want to go where they feel safe."[102]

These statements provide a clear portrait of the obstacles that have fundamentally stifled economic engagement between Iran and the West. On the one side, there is the Iranian regime's behavior, including support for terrorism, continued aggressive policies

---

[101] Official translation of the speech, Khamenei, March 20, 2016. (http://english. khamenei.ir/news/3550/Islamic-Republic-Has-Destroyed-Enemy-Trenches-Inside-Iran)

[102] Press Conference, April 1, 2016. (https://obamawhitehouse.archives.gov/the-press-office/2016/04/01/press-conference-president-obama-412016)

towards regional countries, manufacture and testing of ballistic missiles in contravention of UN Security Council resolution 2231, and systematic egregious human rights violations inside Iran. From the other side, western banks and companies continue to harbor mistrust and doubt, and remain cautious about the high risk of doing business in Iran.

On May 12, 2016, then U.S. Secretary of State John Kerry sought to soothe concerns in a meeting in London with the representatives of nine large European banks, but could not convince them to deal with Iran,[103] in part because in addition to restrictions on dollar transactions, the U.S. has kept in place a range of sanctions enacted prior to the July 2015 nuclear agreement. As a result, banks remain anxious about facing fines by the U.S.[19] It has not been forgotten that in 2014, France's BNP agreed to pay a record $9B in fines for sanctions violations, in "a severe punishment aimed at sending a clear message to other financial institutions around the world," according to Reuters.[104]

Stuart A. Levey, chief legal officer of HSBC, wrote in the Wall Street Journal in 2016 after meeting with Kerry that "HSBC has no intention of doing any new business involving Iran." He added, "There are no assurances as to how such activity would subsequently be viewed by US regulatory and law-enforcement authorities" and so "for these reasons HSBC has no intention of doing any new business involving Iran."[105]

Standard Chartered said in a statement around the same time that it "would not accept any new Iranian clients and would not perform transactions with anyone inside the country."[106] Similarly, Germany's Deutsche Bank said that it "continues to generally restrict business connected to Iran."[107]

[103] HSBC criticises John Kerry over business with Iran request, The Guardian, May 23, 2016 (https://www.theguardian.com/business/2016/may/13/hsbc-criticises-john-kerry-business-iran-europe-banks)

[104] Reuters, July 1, 2014 (http://www.reuters.com/article/us-bnp-paribas-settlement-idUSKBN0F52HA20140701)

[105] The Wall Street Journal, May 12, 2016 (http://www.wsj.com/articles/kerrys-peculiar-message-about-iran-for-european-banks-1463093348)

[106] CNN Money, May 12, 2016. (http://money.cnn.com/2016/05/12/news/iran-banks-europe-john-kerry/)

[107] Ibid.

INSURMOUNTABLE RISKS

The status quo presents numerous political and legal risks to foreign entities looking at the prospect of doing business with Iran. Some of these risks include:

☑ A dramatically high risk of involvement in financial corruption (especially bribery), thereby incurring risk of severe fines for investors as a result of the U.S. regulatory environment, including the Foreign Corruption Practices Act, and similarly the Bribery Act in the United Kingdom.

☑ Risks related to arms sales in view of the Iranian regime's active supplying of arms to the Assad dictatorship in Syria and various militias and terrorist groups in the Middle East. This poses serious risks, especially for private companies involved in providing security services. Similarly, the telecommunications and intelligence technology and communications sectors face sensitive challenges.

☑ In view of the repeated resolutions in the UN General Assembly condemning human rights violations in Iran, the most recent of which was adopted in December 2016,[108] those who deal with the Iranian regime risk providing the actual means of torture, suppression, communications monitoring and internet filtering to a brutal dictatorship.

☑ Internet and digital companies dealing with Iran run the risk of violating regulations regarding ensuring Internet impartiality, freedom of speech, and protection of individual privacy. They also risk unavoidable involvement in activities promoting violence and hatred towards various religious followers, women and oppressed ethnic minorities.

☑ Foreign investors or exporters are obliged to comply with procedures such as ensuring due diligence in the context of international standards stipulated in UN guidelines on business and human rights as well as the Organisation for Economic Co-operation and Development's guidelines for the activities

---

[108] UN General Assembly, December 19, 2016 (https://www.un.org/press/en/2016/ga11879.doc.htm)

of multi-national corporations. It is very unlikely that in the current situation, companies can exercise "due diligence" with respect to dealings with Iran.

☑ A key risk for companies wanting to do business with Iran is association with money-laundering operations, which are systematically conducted by Iranian banks and companies.

☑ There is also the risk of direct or indirect transactions with enterprises or institutions involved in funding terrorism, including groups like Hezbollah. In January 2016, the U.S. formally announced the adoption of the "Hizballah International Financing Prevention Act of 2015," which had become law in December 2015.[109] In June 2016, when at the U.S.'s request the Lebanese Central Bank closed about 100 bank accounts associated with Hezbollah, the leader of the group Hassan Nasrallah publicly brushed off the U.S. sanctions, saying, "We do not have any business projects or investments via banks." Insisting the group "will not be affected," he added, "We are open about the fact that Hezbollah's budget, its income, its expenses, everything it eats and drinks, its weapons and rockets, are from the Islamic Republic of Iran. ... As long as Iran has money, we have money. ... Just as we receive the rockets that we use to threaten Israel, we are receiving our money."[110]

☑ And there is the additional risk that trade will be conducted with companies funding the Iranian regime's Qods Force, which could invite fines and other punitive measures by the U.S. For example, in May 2015, the U.S. Treasury targeted two regional companies in this regard. "The U.S. Treasury said the sanctions applied to Iraq-based Al-Naser Airlines as well as UAE-based Sky Blue Bird Aviation for providing support to Iranian airline Mahan Air," Reuters reported.[111] Mahan Air was previously designated in October 2011 pursuant to E.O. 13224 for providing financial, material, and technological support to the IRGC-Qods Force (IRGC-QF).[112]

---

[109] https://www.congress.gov/bill/114th-congress/house-bill/2297

[110] Agence France Presse, June 25, 2016.

[111] Reuters, May 21, 2015 (http://uk.reuters.com/article/iran-nuclear-sanctions-idUKL1N0YCoZS20150521).

[112] https://www.treasury.gov/press-center/press-releases/Pages/tg1322.aspx

THREATS AND RESTRICTIONS

We can summarize the plethora of threats and restrictions facing foreign investors as well as those choking the ruling regime in Iran:

• INTERNATIONAL:

- ☑ U.S. ban on dollar transactions with the Iranian regime.

- ☑ Developments following the 2016 U.S. presidential elections, which are expected in some fashion to end or decelerate any previous trends of easing restrictions on Iran.

- ☑ Congressional opposition to doing business with Iran in general, and legislation related to fighting terrorism, restrictions on ballistic missiles, and human rights violations.

- ☑ Inclusion of the names of legal entities and officials of the Iranian regime on the U.S. and European Union sanctions lists.

- ☑ Concerns about new sanctions being implemented through the "snapback" mechanism envisioned in the nuclear agreement.

- ☑ European banks' concerns regarding U.S. sanctions and fines.

• DOMESTIC:

- ☑ A bankrupt government and an economy in recession.

- ☑ High rates of delinquency and bankruptcy in the financial system.

- ☑ The virtually absolute domination of the IRGC, security organizations and *bonyads* (foundations) over the country's economy.

- ☑ The regime's financial support for terrorism, especially for the Lebanese Hezbollah.

- ☑ Iran's extremely low ranking on the international scale with regard to ease of doing business.

- ☑ Pervasive corruption, aspects of which are subject to violations of U.S. and European laws, including systematic money-laundering and a lack of any legal framework in which to effectively combat it.

☑ Lack of genuine competition in Iran.

☑ Lack of adequate infrastructure for communications and transportation.

☑ Lack of transparency with respect to a vast portion of the Iranian economy.

☑ Lack of guarantees or secure laws and regulations.

☑ A high-profile, serious power struggle at the top of the regime's hierarchy, which will worsen in the run-up to the presidential elections in May 2017 and beyond.

☑ Extensive social disenchantment, which could lead to wide-ranging public protests, spelling further insecurity and instability for the regime.

CONCLUSION

The last chairman of the Management and Planning Organization in the government of Mohammad Khatami, Hamid-Reza Baradaran Shoraka, declared in the final days of Khatami's tenure in 2005 that about 35 percent of the Iranian economy's labor and financial markets were managed by the semi-government sector. According to a Ministry of Economic Affairs and Finance report, cited earlier, more than 90 percent of asset transfers occurred in the period after 2005, with the bulk of the transfers going to the "non-government public sector." In view of these and other similar facts and figures, it can be estimated that at least 50 percent of the GDP lies in this sector.[113]

Because the IRGC is but one of the financial empires run by the Supreme Leader, the conjecture that over half of Iran's GDP is controlled by institutions controlled by the Supreme Leader is undeniably credible. All these entities are tax-exempt. Some of them, including the IRGC, the State Security Forces, the *Bassij*, the Department of Defense, *Shahid* Foundation, and *Emdad* Committee also receive funding from the annual government budget.

However, the astronomical profits they make from their banks and subsidiaries deviate from the stream of government revenues. They are not spent on the country's needs or infrastructure. Rather, these funds are spent on mechanisms to control and suppress the population at home and to export war and terrorism abroad. At the same time, an additional 25 to 30 percent of the annual budget is spent on the regime's domestic suppression and regional

---

[113] In a February 15, 2010 report, The Guardian noted that the IRGC "has grown into a behemoth which dominates both Iran's official and black economies. It is impossible to gauge its market share, but western estimates range from a third to nearly two-thirds of Iran's GDP – amounting to tens of billions of dollars."

machinations. Therefore, the claim that the Iranian regime's military expenses do not surpass two to three percent of the budget is extremely naïve, assuming that it is not politically motivated.[114]

"RELIGIOUS FOUNDATIONS" PART AND PARCEL OF KHAMENEI'S EMPIRE

IRGC Brig. Gen. Parviz Fattah
in Karbala (Beinolharamein)

There are, of course, those who choose to assume that these affluent foundations, some of whose assets were listed above, constitute "religious foundations" that are to some degree independent of the Iranian regime. Based on the evidence and details provided in this manuscript, however, these foundations are entirely controlled by the *velayat-e faqih* (Supreme Leader). To illustrate this point, we need only refer to the fact that Khamenei personally handpicks the heads of the *Shahid*, *Mostazafan* and *Setad* foundations. In addition, he appoints the chairman and the entire board of the *Emdad* Committee.

In April 2015, Khamenei appointed Parviz Fattah as the chairman of the *Emdad* Committee. Fattah is an IRGC brigadier general, who was the director of the IRGC Cooperative Foundation for five years. Prior to that, he was the deputy director of Khatam al-Anbiya Headquarters. With this appointment, the lengthy rule of the *Mo'talefeh* faction over the *Emdad* Committee ended, and the committee is now entirely in the hands of Khamenei.[115]

---

[114] See, for example, "Is Iran really one of the world's best investments?" *Financial Times*, March 11, 2016 <https://www.ft.com/content/ 7349a988-e6f7-11e5-bc31-138df2ae9ee6>

[115] The *Mo'talefeh* faction is part of the ruling coalition and defends the *velayat-e faqih*, but since its leadership is comprised of veteran Bazaar merchants, the group was in some cases slowing down the implementation of Khamenei's aggressive strategy in recent years.

Furthermore, the placement of Fattah at the helm of the committee was especially designed to steer the committee's resources towards the war in Syria.

In March 2016, mullah Abbas Vaez Tabasi, the powerful custodian of the *Astan-e Qods Razavi* Foundation, died. In the context of the regime's factional infighting, he had leaned closer to Khamenei's rivals. Khamenei appointed mullah Ebrahim Raeesi to replace him as the custodian of the Foundation, thereby solidifying his domination over all the major *bonyads* (foundations). Raeesi is one of the most significant players responsible for the massacre of over 30,000 political prisoners in 1988.

Ebrahim Raeesi, custodian of the Astan-e Qods Razavi Foundation

The Iranian regime is on the one hand comprised of civic ministries and other institutions that form a part of the executive branch, while on the other hand it includes the Supreme Leader's office as well as the array of military, security and financial institutions and those involved in the export of fundamentalism. Applying the term "non-governmental" or "public sector" to the latter would indicate academic naiveté, or more ominously, willful deception designed to hide the real character of a suppressive fundamentalist regime that has amassed astronomical wealth.

WESTERN INVESTORS PLAYING THE NAME GAME

Western companies engaged in economic and financial deals with Iran portray their activities as transactions with the "private sector." This is a baseless, hollow claim. As shown by the data provided, behind the official banks and companies lies a web of institutions controlled by the theocracy, and specifically the IRGC. For example, in September 2015, the French hotel company Accor signed a contract with the Iranian company Aria Ziggurat to manage the two 4-and-5-star hotel chains of Ibis and Novotel.[116] Aria Ziggurat is owned 100 percent by a tourism investment firm called SEMGA (Iran Cultural Heritage and Tourism Investment Group Co.). It is one of the investment entities owned by the IRGC.

Sebastien Bazin, chairman and CEO of AccorHotels, a French hotel chain, second left, and Mehdi Jahangiri, chairman of Iran's Aria Ziggurat Tourism Development Company, shake hands while exchanging their agreement documents at a newly build Novotel hotel in Tehran, Iran, Tuesday, Sept. 15, 2015.

---

[116] http://www.usnews.com/news/business/articles/2015/09/15/iran-firm-signs-branding-deal-with-french-hotel-chain

Another example involves a company called KBC, which has exclusive rights for the sale in Iran of products of the French company Sanofi Pasteur.[117] KBC is part of the *Barkat* Pharmaceutical holding company, one of the most profitable holding companies owned by Khamenei's *Setad*. KBC has also signed an imports contract with Germany's Sandoz Hexal. It has also signed cooperation agreements with representatives from Britain's GSK and U.S.-based Jansen companies.[118]

The *Sobhan* Pharmaceutical company (which produces pills) is owned by the *Setad's Barkat* Pharmaceutical holding; it has signed agreements with the Italian ABC Pharmaceutical for the licensed production of Ursobil-250 pills. It has also signed an agreement with Poland's Adamed Group for the licensed manufacturing of the drug Contrahist.

Another company belonging to the *Setad* foundation is *Alborz Balak*, a producer of drug ingredients. The company has agreements with India's Dr. Reddy.

Ati Farmed, another company tied to the foundation, was created in 2011 through joint investments with the Swiss Strategen company to produce hormone pills.

The *Kowsar* Agricultural Industries and Mechanization Company (owned by the *Kowsar* Economic Organization of the *Shahid* Foundation) has obtained the Italian company SKA's exclusive rights in Iran to design and construct structures for poultry farming.

Kowsar also has obtained exclusive rights from the Dutch Invetech for custom automation of egg incubators. Additionally, it has exclusive rights for Belgium's Petersime in Iran. Petersime develops incubators and hatcheries. Belgium's Poultec has signed agreements with this company as well.

The *Kowsar* Agriculture Investment Company (owned by the *Shahid* Foundation) closely cooperates with the French company Midatest in the field of livestock farming.

In fact, as reported by an investigative journalist in Iran working for the French daily Le Monde, "There are no significant enterprises in Iran other than those controlled by the IRGC and religious foundations."[119]

---

[117] http://www.bpharmed.com/en/article/p66-K-B-C-Trading-Co

[118] http://www.bpharmed.com/en/article/p49-Introduction

[119] Le Monde, April 22, 2016

ECONOMIC DOMINANCE TO FUND SUPPRESSION, WAR AND TERRORISM

The monopoly of the overwhelming and most influential portions of the Iranian economy by the Supreme Leader's office and its affiliated institutions has been obtained by seizing ownership of property from Iranian society. The profits generated from these excessive transfers of wealth are on the one hand funding domestic suppression, war, terrorism and meddling in the countries of the region; and, on the other hand, they provide the means by which the regime exerts financial leverage and incentives to acquire the support of a small portion of the Iranian society. As a result of the clerical regime's rule, the Iranian people have been deprived of economic opportunities and are in essence under "sanctions" imposed by the *velayat-e faqih*.

A breakdown of where Iran funds terror

A STRATEGIC IMPASSE

The vast and interconnected network of wealth and power in the hands of the *velayat-e faqih* is indicative of a sophisticated monopoly over the Iranian economy. Doing business with Iran is to do business with Khamenei and the IRGC. At the same time, the significant revenues from this monopoly enable and primarily fund the regime's terrorism, intransigence and regional adventurism.

Meanwhile, the above facts and figures show that the regime is strategically unstable as a result of these developments:

☑ It has been unable to keep pace with the demands of a growing population and a young demographic. According to The Economist, "The Islamic Republic's labor force is expected to grow by 2.5% annually in the five years to 2020, equivalent to about 3 million new job seekers. The problem is thorniest for young people and women, for whom unemployment stands at 25.2% and 19.7% respectively." These figures are, in part, obtained from official and ultra-conservative estimates. The real picture is much "thornier."

☑ Tehran has not been able to create the required number of net new jobs despite the lifting of a majority of sanctions in 2015;[20]

☑ At the same time, the options for expansionary policies are limited, which means Tehran faces major constraints to revive the economy after a recession;

☑ Dramatically falling oil prices have slashed budgetary commitments and the ability to pay for infrastructure needs;

☑ Future security uncertainties for the regime have multiplied as a result of a lower currency reserve;

☑ Meanwhile, the 38-year-old economic mismanagement has taken new proportions with the Supreme Leader and the IRGC being more involved. Corruption is at an all-time high. The 2016 Index of Economic Freedom puts Iran almost 20% lower than the world average when it comes to freedom to corruption measures.[120] The report says, "Corruption is

---

[120] See 2016 Index of Economic Freedom: <http://www.heritage.org/index/visualize?cnts=iran&type=9>

pervasive. The hardline clerical establishment has gained great wealth through control of tax-exempt foundations that dominate many economic sectors."

☑ The inflation rate has been spiraling out of control despite some minor efforts to arrest the worsening trend. Both the unemployment rate and the inflation rate are enduring and persistent, resulting in profound structural damages.

This disastrous economic situation is the most enduring long-term source for social discontent, hence a major source of instability for the regime at home. Unemployed youth and women, recent university grads, workers, civic employees, and many others are looking for minimum sources of subsistence. That has created a vulnerable situation for the regime as protests are on the rise and they could lead to a massive upheaval, similar cases of which were seen during the Arab Spring uprisings in the broader region.

This extreme monopoly has also created tailwinds upon which the regime's foreign adventurism has intensified, but within the regime's own ranks it has created a sense of chaos. From an economic viewpoint, it has accelerated the waste and squander of Iran's economic resources, leading to a greater recession, more unemployment and extensive poverty among the population.

These excesses have occurred by depriving the society of the ownership of its wealth by means of force. As noted in reference to articles of the regime's constitution, any form of coexistence, peace or engagement between Iran's rulers and Iranian society at large has eroded, leaving only room for permanent tension between the two sides. Moreover, the monopolization itself translates into circumstances that create enormous hurdles to true economic growth and development in Iran.

In other words, the *velayat-e faqih* has amassed its wealth by robbing the Iranian people of theirs, while violating their rights. In the process, and thus, the regime has eradicated the social backing and support instrumental and necessary for a government's stability and legitimacy. That has made Tehran more vulnerable than ever before. As social demands grow in breadth and depth, the regime's ability to respond to those demands appears increasingly limited. That is a recipe for a major social transformation, one that certainly excludes a possible future role for Tehran's theocratic rulers.

ENDNOTES

1 Provision 9 of the First Development Program Bill states: "In implementing Article 147 of the Constitution to leverage the expertise and capabilities of the armed forces, the defense department and the logistics of the armed forces for the rebuilding of the country, the executive units above shall be permitted, in view of the expertise, capabilities, abilities and potentials of the forces under their control, to sign contracts with the executive for the implementation of construction projects and designs." Moreover, according to the Bassij Organization Authority Reforms Bill, adopted in 2007 by the parliament (Majlis): "In line with the implementation of Article 147 of the Islamic Republic of Iran Constitution, the Construction Bassij Organization and its affiliates are considered to be among the executors of public and government plans. They are permitted to engage in contracts or agreements with executive branch institutions." The Urban Land Bill, Article 1, has made reference to Article 31 of the Constitution to justify land grabs and confiscations.

2 Text of Khamenei's order related to the "general policies of the cooperative sector":

1. Increasing the share of the cooperative sector in the national economy to 25 percent by the end of the Fifth Five-Year Development Plan.

2. Effective measures by the government to establish cooperatives for the unemployed with a view to generating productive employment.

3. Support by the government to set up and promote cooperatives by offering incentives such as tax concessions, providing concessional credit facilities by all financial institutions, abstaining from receiving any additional levies or other charges in excess of those paid by the private sector.

4. Removal of all barriers and constraints that obstruct the presence of the cooperative sector in all economic arenas, including banking and insurance.

5. Establishment of the Cooperative Development Bank funded by the government for the purpose of enhancing the share of the cooperative sector in the national economy.

6. Support by the government to enable cooperatives to gain market access and providing this sector full information on non-discriminatory basis.

7. Exercise of the right of sovereignty of the government in the framework of policy-making and overseeing the enforcement of the applicable laws and avoiding interference in the administrative and management affairs of the cooperatives.

8. Development of technical and vocational training and other supportive programmes with a view to enhancing efficiency and empowerment of the cooperatives.

9. Flexibility and diversity in methods of raising capital, distribution of shareholding in the cooperative sector and taking necessary measures that set in motion establishment of new cooperatives in addition to the conventional ones in the form of public joint stock companies with fixed limits of shareholding, the ceiling for which will be determined by law.

10. Support by the government of the cooperatives, proportionate to the number of members.

11. Establishment of nationwide cooperatives to cover the three lowest deciles of the population with a view to poverty alleviation.

http://eng.tpo.ir/index.aspx?siteid=5&pageid=1940

3 The Entekhab news website said on June 9, 2015, "The president's first deputy, Ishaq Jahangiri, said: one of the elements of Article 44 was the issue of transfers. They did this through all those mechanisms and got the money, and we don't know what happened. 100 billion dollars was sold from telecommunications shares to refineries, to factors and copper mines." The Mizan news agency said on January 4, 2015, "The Minister of Roads and Urban Development said that instead of real privatization, we released state assets, and added: 100 billion dollars has been privatized, but no one knows where it went." The ISNA news agency reported on January 4, 2015, "Abbas Akhundi (minister of roads and urban development) said: ... over the past 10 years, 100 billion dollars worth of assets have been privatized. But, it is unclear where this money has gone to and how it was managed. There is a halo of uncertainty around it."

4 The number of banks and financial and credit institutions have been categorized on the central bank's website: 3 government commerce banks, 5 specialized government-owned banks, 20 non-government-owned banks, 2 "*Gharzolhasaneh*" banks (non-profit granting funds), 1 bi-national bank, 158 cooperative credit companies, 821 legal credit cooperatives, 35 leasing companies, 434 credible and licensed currency exchange offices, 7 bank *Gharzolhasaneh* funds and credit institutions, and 4 credit institutions. (Central Bank website, <http://www.cbi.ir/simplelist/1541.aspx>)

It has also been reported that close to 7,000 illegal *Gharzolhasaneh* boxes and credit cooperatives operate outside the supervision of the central bank (Naft News and Analysis, quoting Hamid Tehranfar, deputy director of supervision of the central bank, at the government and private sector cooperation conference, May 12, 2015) .

5 The central bank issued a statement on January 20, 2014, saying: The total amount of loans is about $165B. Non-performing loans are valued at $25.5B, accounting for close to 15 percent of total loans. In 61 cases, the loans were above $31.5M each, of which $4.8B was non-performing, translating into 19 percent of the total in bad loans in the banking network. 112 cases had $15.7M to $31.5M each, of which a total of about $2.4B was non-performing. This translates into 10 percent of the total worth of bad loans in the banking network. Therefore, according to the central bank report, roughly 29 percent of the bad loans in the banking network is owed by 173 individuals or legal entities in the country (Central Bank website, <http://cbi.ir/showitem/11406.aspx>)

6 Following growing tensions between the Majlis and the government over the adoption of this law, which culminated with Ahmadinejad threatening to put the issue to "a referendum to resolve the conflict between the two branches," on March 21, 2010, Khamenei publicly intervened and called on all three branches to "maintain unity when it comes to important decisions." He also warned that "disagreements should not produce a halt in the country's advance nor should they induce individuals to separate their paths." Khamenei's intervention was in reality to tip the balance of power in favor of Ahmadinejad's government. On April 5, 2010, Khamenei firmly supported Ahmadinejad's views regarding the elimination of subsidies and called on all three branches to maintain their unity in decision making. And, on April 18, 2010, after Khamenei's intervention, the parliament (Majlis) affirmed the Ahmadinejad government's views during a meeting behind closed doors.

7 With respect to the costs of the Syrian war, which has weighted on the Iranian economy since 2011, the following reports and information are instructive:

On May 28, 2013, Adib Mialeh, the head of Syria's central bank, spoke of two lines of credit worth about $4B opened by the Iranian regime for the Syrian government. He also mentioned a loan of about $3B from the regime.

On September 4, 2014, French daily *Le Figaro* reported that Tehran had opened a $4B line of credit for the Assad regime.

On July 8, 2015, Syria's official news agency, SANA, reported, "The Syrian President, Bashar Assad, has approved a new law accepting a $1B credit from its regional ally Iran."

On December 20, 2014, Reuters quoted a Syrian trade official as saying, "'If it had not been for Iranian support we could not have survived the crisis,' a senior Syrian trade official said from Damascus, requesting anonymity." The Reuters report adds, "In July last year, Iran granted Syria a $3.6 billion credit facility to buy oil products, according to officials and bankers at the time. Another $1 billion went for non-oil products."

On May 7, 2015, the state-run *Sharq* estimated that "Iran, China and Russia help Syria with $500M monthly through the sale of oil and provision of credit lines to Syria."

On April 27, 2015, *Christian Science Monitor* noted, " Diplomatic sources in Beirut estimate that Iran spends between $1 billion and $2 billion a month in Syria in cash handouts and military support." The paper went on to say, "Staffan de Mistura, the United Nations envoy to Syria, recently told a private gathering in Washington that Iran has been channeling as much as $35 billion a year into Syria, according to one of the participants at the meeting."

In a meeting at the French Senate on May 5, 2015, Nazir Hakim, the General Secretary of the Political Bureau of the Syrian National Coalition, said, "In my view, Assad would only stay in power if the Iranian regime continues its support for him. Based on credible data, $87B has been spent over a three-year period. Unless and until the Iranian regime leaves Syria, Assad will not leave power."

8 The French daily *Le Figaro* wrote on October 8, 2013, "Over the past 30 years, Iran has given more than $30B to the Lebanese Hezbollah. The leader of Hezbollah Seyyed Hassan Nasrallah said in 2012: 'His Excellency Imam Khamenei said on Friday explicitly that the Islamic Republic supports resistance movements in Lebanon and Palestine, and we do not want anything in return because we are just fulfilling our religious duties. This is the first time that the most senior figure in the Islamic Republic speaks so clearly and explicitly in this regard. ... Following this speech, everyone would be speaking on their own behalf. I'm speaking on Hezbollah's behalf. Yes, we received moral, and political and material support in all possible forms from the Islamic Republic of Iran since 1982. In the past we used to tell half the story and stay silent on the other half. We said there is moral and political support but when they asked us about the material and financial and military support we were silent. We did not want to embarrass our brothers in Iran. But now that the highest official (Khamenei) says that they support us, we must speak openly. ... It is a source of pride for the Islamic Republic in Iran to give this support because it was the Lebanese resistance that realized the greatest and most important Arab victory against Israel on May 25, 2000. If it were not for the moral and material support of Iran for the resistance movement in Lebanon, this victory would not have been achievable.'" (Al-Alam Arab TV, February 7, 2012). See also Reuters, February 7, 2012. <http://www.reuters.com/article/us-lebanon-hezbollah-idUSTRE81629H20120207>

9 In April 2013, two American research institutes, the Carnegie Endowment for International Peace and the Federation of American Scientists said in a joint report that the nuclear program's cost—measured in lost foreign investment and oil revenue—has been well over $100 billion. Other experts report higher figures. An Iranian economist has estimated the total number to be $600B to $700B. Mehran Mostafavi, a university professor in France, says, "Estimates obtained from what officials and international institutions have said show that the costs imposed on Iran as a result of the nuclear program surpasses the cost of the eight-year war with Iraq. ... Experts estimate that at least $600B to $700B has been invested directly. There are also indirect costs, including the brain drain, the opportunity loss of drilling joint oil and gas fields, and the inability to sell oil. If we account for all this, then we can estimate the real costs to be well over $2 trillion" (Radio Zamaneh, translated from Farsi, February 6, 2014).

One of Ahmadinejad's ministers of labour, Mohammad Jahromi, put the real number even higher. He said in an interview in 2014 with the Nameh News website, "The nuclear program costs the country over $160B per year to maintain."

On July 5, 2014, a former regime nuclear negotiator, Hossein Mousavian, said in an interview with *Sharq* daily, "The direct and indirect costs of the nuclear projects are estimated to top several hundred billion dollars."

The *Economist* said in a May 12, 2014 that the program has cost Iran "upwards of $300 billion by some estimates." (http://www.economist.com/blogs/economist-explains/2014/05/economist-explains-5) If we consider the starting point of the large-scale development of the nuclear program to be the construction of the Natanz site, the costs of this program over the past 20 years, on the basis of the above reports and figures, has been anywhere between $5B to $30B per year. Even conservative estimates would put the number closer to $10B/year.

10 I. Due to the weaknesses of the ground forces, the insufficient number of IRGC forces, and the severe vulnerabilities of the air force, which has not been modernized since the ouster of the Shah in 1979, the expansion of missile stockpiles has an important place in the regime's strategy.

Currently, the Iranian regime produces a variety of missiles, including short-range ballistic missiles (Shahab 1, Shahab 2, Fateh 110, Nazeat), medium-range ballistic missiles (Shahab 3, Fajr 3, Qadr, Seyjal 2), anti-ship missiles (Nour, Kowsar, Raad), and anti-ship ballistic missiles (Tondar, Khalij Fars), among others.

In addition, the mullahs have set up a costly stockpile for the Lebanese Hezbollah while equipping Hamas with Fateh missiles.

11 The New York Times on June 22, 2011 wrote about the development of a public rift between Khamenei and Ahmadinejad: "Since April, an unusually public battle has escalated between two men long seen as ideological soul mates— Mr. Ahmadinejad and the supreme leader, Ayatollah Ali Khamenei. Former staunch conservative allies among the clergy, in Parliament and in the military, have abandoned the president in droves, voicing their allegiance to Ayatollah Khamenei while labeling the presidential circle a "deviant current." ... It started in April, when Mr. Ahmadinejad tried to fire Heydar Moslehi, the intelligence minister, and the supreme leader ordered him reinstated. Mr. Ahmadinejad pouted at home for 11 days, returning only after the supreme leader signaled that the president, too, could be replaced. Mr. Ahmadinejad was elected twice using Ayatollah Khamenei's political machine. But he wanted to build his own patronage system and source of funds, separate from the intelligence network loyal to the supreme leader, to elect candidates in the 2012 parliamentary elections and most important, in the 2013 presidential race, according to Iran experts." <http://www.nytimes.com/2011/06/23/world/middleeast/23iran.html>

The Guardian reported around the same time that: "Ahmadinejad's unprecedented disobedience prompted harsh criticism from conservatives who warned that he might face the fate of Abdulhassan Banisadr, Iran's first post-revolution president who was impeached and exiled for allegedly attempting to undermine clerical power. Ayatollah Mesbah Yazdi, a hardline cleric close to Khamenei, warned that disobeying the supreme leader – who has the ultimate power in Iran – is equivalent to "apostasy from God"." <https://www.theguardian.com/world/2011/may/05/ahmadinejad-allies-charged-with-sorcery>.

The Guardian added, "Several people said to be close to the president and his chief of staff, Esfandiar Rahim Mashaei, have been arrested in recent days and charged with being "magicians" and invoking djinns (spirits)."

And, this year, Khamenei advised Ahmadinejad not to run for president. <http://www.nytimes.com/2016/09/27/world/middleeast/iran-ayatollah-ali-khamenei-mahmoud-ahmadinejad.html?_r=0>

This is while in 2009 Khamenei had publicly said – despite Ahmadinejad's unpopularity – that his views were "closer to Ahmadinejad's." http://www.pbs.org/wgbh/pages/frontline/tehranbureau/ 2011/07/khamenei-versus-khameneiwill-ahmadinejad-be-impeached.html

12 In 2005, Ahmadinejad rose to power through a coalition with Khamenei against Ali Akbar Hashemi Rafsanjani. However, the loose coalition of pro-Khamenei and pro-Ahmadinejad factions began to collapse in the ensuing years. In 2012, the supreme leader's loyalists won the majority of seats in parliament. According to Reuters on March 4, 2012: "Clerical Supreme Leader Ayatollah Ali Khamenei has tightened his grip on Iran's faction-ridden politics after loyalists won over 75 percent of seats in parliamentary elections at the expense of President Mahmoud Ahmadinejad, a near-complete count showed. The widespread defeat of Ahmadinejad supporters – including his sister, Parvin Ahmadinejad – is expected to reduce the president to a lame duck after he sowed divisions by challenging the utmost authority of Khamenei in the governing hierarchy. ... The results are hard to compare with the outgoing parliament since Khamenei and Ahmadinejad loyalists were united in the 2008 legislative elections, garnering about 70 percent of seats." <http://www.reuters.com/article/us-iran-election-result-idUSTRE82306420120304>.

After the rift, Khamenei's faction accused Ahmadinejad's faction of harbouring a "deviant current." The divisions strengthened during the 2012 parliamentary elections. However, they were more firmly on display during the 2013 presidential elections. According to Reuters in March 2013, "Last month Parliament Speaker Ali Larijani – also a principalist – was pelted with shoes and stones by Ahmadinejad supporters in the holy city of Qom, where he had come to make a speech on the 34th anniversary of Iran's revolution." <http://www.reuters.com/article/us-iran-election-idUSBRE92I0HY20130319> Even Khamenei's "Principalists" faction was divided.

Al-Monitor reported in 2013 after the presidential elections: "Iran's hard-liners, known domestically as Principalists, are off balance for the first time in nine years following their devastating landslide defeat to political centrist Hassan Rouhani. The president-elect won with 51% of the votes, millions of which came from Reformists, who were mobilized en masse to elect who they saw as their best hope for change. Principalists Mohammad Bagher Ghalibaf, the mayor of Tehran, and Saeed Jalili, Iran's arch-conservative nuclear negotiator, accrued 17% and 11% of the vote, respectively. The 2013 election will likely be the death knell for the Principalist coalition, created in 2002 to wrest control of the country away from the then-dominant Reformist bloc that had consolidated power under former presidents Hashemi Rafsanjani and Mohammad Khatami. Following the Principalists' foray into mainstream politics in the 2004 parliamentary elections, they swept to power on the landslide runoff victory of Mahmoud Ahmadinejad in 2005. Over the course of Ahmadinejad's eight years in office— with the help of rulings on pesky Reformists from the conservative Guardian Council— the camp successfully purged Reformists from the body politic of Iran. But the election of Rouhani has turned the tide on the Principalists, revealing them to be little more than a bitterly divided and dysfunctional rabble." "This is a crisis of the current political narrative of the Principalists," said Walter Posch of the German Institute for International and Security Affairs in

Berlin. "Their finest hour was the 2005 election of Mahmoud Ahmadinejad. Ever since then, they have tried to get the whole country into their hands, but they failed."

<http://www.al-monitor.com/pulse/originals/2013/06/iran-hard-liners-decline.html#ixzz4Plh6M4I2>

13 Ali Akbar Hashemi Rafsanjani, one of the most senior officials of the Iranian regime, is widely seen as leading a rival faction to Khamenei's. When his presidential bid was rejected by the Khamenei-appointed Guardian Council in 2013, the New York Times wrote: "Tuesday's disqualification also seemed like an official repudiation of [Rafsanjani's] ideas of a liberal economy and more freedoms." (Although the assessment that Rafsanjani seeks "more freedoms" is loose at best, the sentiment expressed in this sentence still points to the fact that Rafsanjani represents a different streak than Khamenei when it comes to tactics and methods. In relation to strategic ambitions for the regime's survival, however, both men remain on the same page. It is only in the realm of distributing power and wealth where they lock horns).

Still, Khamenei's direct assault on the leader of his rival faction, Rafsanjani, was indicative of his intent to marginalize challengers and monopolize power as much as possible during the Ahmadinejad years. He made significant attempts in this regard, but failed in 2013 to complete the endeavour.

Khamenei had gone so far in the policy of contraction – and monopolization of power – that there was real talk about abolishing the office of the presidency: " Analysts have long speculated— and some conservative clerics have confirmed— that the ruling faction is determined to abolish the office of president, which has served as a locus of opposition under the populist incumbent, Mahmoud Ahmadinejad, and before him the reformist Mohammad Khatami, who pushed for more personal freedoms. While by no means certain, it is now a greater possibility."

<http://www.nytimes.com/2013/05/22/world/middleeast/iranians-await-list-of-approved-candidates.html>

"Khamenei has marginalized Rafsanjani since the centrist former president lent tacit support in 2009 to opposition leaders who declared that Ahmadinejad's re-election was rigged, touching off the worst unrest since the 1979 Islamic Revolution." <http://www.reuters.com/article/us-iran-election-velayati-idUSBRE95B09420130612>.

During the 2013 presidential elections, the dominant perception was that one of Khamenei's candidates would win the election. The New York Times, for example, reported in the days leading up to the election, "Barring further surprises, the winner of the June election will now be drawn from a slate of conservative candidates in Iran's ruling camp, a loose alliance of Shiite Muslim clerics and Revolutionary Guard commanders." < http://www.nytimes.com/2013/05/22/world/middleeast/iranians-await-list-of-approved-candidates.html>

Similarly, the British daily Guardian said, Hassan Rouhani is "a reformist who is seen as having little chance of victory." <https://www.theguardian.com/world/2013/may/21/iran-presidential-election-rafsanjani-disqualified>

These evaluations were expressed in the context of Khamenei's onslaught on Rafsanjani's camp and even family. In the run-up to the election, one of Rafsanjani's daughters was jailed for six months. <http://www.nytimes.com/2013/05/22/world/middleeast/iranians-await-list-of-approved-candidates.html>. His son and confidant, Mehdi, has been under attack by the judiciary since 2012. < http://www.reuters.com/article/us-iran-rafsanjani-son-idUSKBN0MB0SF20150315>. In September 2012, "Iran's state news agency [said] authorities have detained the son of influential ex-president Akbar Hashemi Rafsanjani two days after arresting the politician's daughter." <https://english.alarabiya.net/articles/2012/09/24/239986.html>

In 2013, Khamenei's Guardian Council banned Rafsanjani, who is seen as leading the rival faction, from running in the 2013 presidential elections. "A former president supported by Iran's moderates and considered a founding member of the Islamic republic was disqualified Tuesday from running in the coming election, generating surprise and tension." <https://www.washingtonpost.com/world/middle_east/iranian-presidential-candidates-announced-rafsanjani-disqualified/2013/05/21/af93f112-c23a-11e2-9642-a56177f1cdf7_story.html>

Prior to that, in 2011, he lost his powerful role as the chairman of the Assembly of Exerts to Khamenei ally Mohammad Reza Mahdavi Kani. The Washington Times said, "Rafsanjani has been losing power gradually over the years step by step. His son, Mohsen, resigned as the head of Tehran subway system after 17 years in office on Friday, citing lack of support from the government." <http://www.washingtontimes.com/news/2011/mar/8/iranian-ex-leader-rafsanjani-loses-powerful-role/>

Still, in the important 2013 presidential elections, Khamenei had to retreat from his ambitions of taking over the office through his allies again, and conceded to Rouhani's presidency. Rouhani is seen more closely aligned with Rafsanjani. In January 2016, Khamenei's Guardian Council also conceded to having Rouhani and Rafsanjani stand in elections for the Assembly of Experts. <http://www.reuters.com/article/us-iran-election-candidates-idUSKCN0V419V>

A *Foreign Affairs* piece summarized these events as such: "Going into the election, a Rouhani victory seemed unlikely. The conservatives' favored candidate was said to be Saeed Jalili, a pious and prim bureaucrat who was appointed as lead nuclear negotiator six years ago. ... It is easy to understand why Jalili was seen as leading the pack; he is basically an improved version of Ahmadinejad. ... given his limited national profile, would be perfectly subservient to Khamenei.

"The conservative camp remained divided, never coalescing around a single candidate. Had it managed to do so, it could have at least forced the election into a run-off.

"After all, the conservatives have held all the cards in Iran since 2005; they dominate its institutions and dictate the terms of the debate. With the leading reformists imprisoned or in exile, no one expected that the forces of change could be revived so powerfully. When his expectations proved off base last Friday, Khamenei could have simply opted not to risk a repeat of 2009.

"The election of Rouhani, a centrist cleric who has been close to Iran's apex of power since the 1979 revolution, is an improbably auspicious end to the Ahmadinejad era."

<https://www.foreignaffairs.com/articles/iran/2013-06-16/why-rouhani-won-and-why-khamenei-let-him>

14 In August 2014, after Nouri al-Maliki's resignation as Iraq's Prime Minister, the BBC reported, "Less than two months ago, Iran's Supreme Leader, Ayatollah Ali Khamenei, spelled out his position on Iraq. Iran was against US intervention, he said, and the world should respect the results of Iraq's April election which saw victory for Nouri Maliki's alliance. But the ayatollah has been overtaken by events. <http://www.bbc.com/news/world-middle-east-28777142>

It is no secret that Tehran was one of Maliki's most ardent supporters, so much so that The Washington Times wrote, "Others say Mr. al-Maliki is acting as a kind of puppet for the neighboring Shiite Islamic Republic of Iran, whose strategic operatives seek to gain as much power as possible over Sunni populations in the region. Long-time intelligence and national security columnist David Ignatius argued last week in The Washington Post that "Iran has waged a brilliant covert-action campaign that turned Maliki and Iraq into virtual clients of Tehran — and in the process alienated Sunnis and pushed them toward extremism." <http://www.washingtontimes.com/news/2014/jan/14/deputy-iraqi-prime-minister-blames-us-al-maliki-fo/>

Tehran never volunteered to give up Maliki. As mentioned in the BBC report, Khamenei had met him 2 months prior to his resignation, standing firmly behind him. But, in the end, the regime could not fend off growing resentment towards its disgraced beneficiary. Ultimately, in August 2014, Maliki said "he had agreed to relinquish power, a move that came after days of crisis in which his deployment of extra security forces around the capital had raised worries of a military coup." < http://www.nytimes.com/2014/08/15/world/middleeast/iraq-prime-minister-.html>

Especially among the Sunnis, Maliki was seen as an Iranian agent. In 2014, The New Yorker reported, "In the protests at Ramadi, a Sunni member of parliament named Ahmed al-Alwani had inflamed the crowds, accusing Maliki of being in league with the Iranian regime, the region's great Shiite power. "My message is for the snake Iran!" Alwani shouted into a microphone, jabbing his finger into the air. Referring to Maliki and those around him as "Safavids" and "Zoroastrians," terms that denote Iranian invaders, he said, "Let them listen up and know that those gathered here will return Iraq to its people!""

Maliki had strong ties to Iran going back to the 1980s. During the Iran-Iraq War, "Maliki stayed in Iran for seven years, fighting against his own country, only to have the war end in stalemate. In the interview with Iraqi television, he said that he lost sixty-three fighters. "Some died inside Iraq and others in Iran," he said. "Their graves are still there."" < http://www.newyorker.com/magazine/2014/04/28/what-we-left-behind>

The New Yorker added, "Most indications are that [Iran] exercises great influence over Maliki's government. A conspicuous example is the airlift of guns and fighters to the Syrian regime of Bashar al-Assad, another Iranian ally. Transport planes flying to Damascus pass unmolested through Iraqi airspace. Maliki insisted that his officials regularly inspect the flights, and that they carry only humanitarian supplies. American officials say that inspections are rare."

<http://www.newyorker.com/magazine/2014/04/28/what-we-left-behind>

Maliki filled cabinet posts with key Tehran allies. The Washington Institute for Near East Policy said in an April 2011 report, "Like Washington, Tehran has discovered that its influence in Iraq has limits. However, the formation of a new government under Prime Minister Nouri al-Maliki that incorporates many of Tehran's closest allies, and the impending U.S. military withdrawal, will present new opportunities for Iran to further expand its influence in Iraq." http://www.washingtoninstitute.org/uploads/Documents/pubs/PolicyFocus111.pdf

In an article published in the Washington Post, Ali Khedery, the longest continuously serving American official in Iraq, chronicled Maliki's tenure and his deep ties to Iran. He said, for example: "With instructions from Tehran, Maliki began to form a cabinet around some of Iran's favorite men in Iraq. Hadi al-Amiri, the notorious Badr Brigade commander, became transportation minister, controlling strategically sensitive sea, air and land ports. Khudair Khuzaie became vice president, later serving as acting president. Abu Mahdi al-Muhandis, the Dawa party mastermind behind the bombing of the U.S. Embassy in Kuwait in 1983, became an adviser to Maliki and his neighbor in the Green Zone. Hundreds, perhaps thousands, of Sadrist detainees were released. And Maliki purged the National Intelligence Service of its Iran division, gutting the Iraqi government's ability to monitor and check its neighboring foe. .... Maliki's most ardent American supporters ignored the warning signs and stood by as an Iranian general decided Iraq's fate in 2010. Ironically, these same officials are now scrambling to save Iraq, yet are refusing to publicly condemn Maliki's abuses and are providing him with arms that he can use to wage war against his political rivals." <https://www.washingtonpost.com/opinions/why-we-stuck-with-maliki--and-lost-iraq/2014/07/03/0dd6a8a4-f7ec-11e3-a606-946fd632f9f1_story.html>

The former President of the European Parliament's Delegation for Relations with Iraq from 2009 to 2014, Struan Stevenson, has chronicled some of Maliki's extensive sectarian and polarizing policies at the behest of the Iranian regime. In one piece, he wrote, "As a puppet of the Iranian mullahs, Maliki took his orders from Tehran. They demanded that he should manipulate the voting lists, banning many Sunnis, anti-Iranians and anti-sectarian politicians from standing for election. They demanded that he should exercise political control over the Iraqi justice system to accuse prominent politicians of being Baathists. They demanded he get rid of all the senior Sunni officials from his own government. This ultimately led to the bogus charges of terrorism leveled against Vice President Tariq al-Hashemi. He avoided arrest by fleeing to Kurdistan and then Turkey, where he now lives. However, 12 of his bodyguards were arrested and confessed to terrorism under torture. One bodyguard was so badly tortured that he died. Amnesty

15 Iran has embroiled itself in the Syrian crisis. It has sent billions of dollars, thousands of troops and large caches of weapons to the war-torn country to help the government of Bashar al-Assad stay in power despite overwhelming protests by the majority of the country. This has come at a catastrophic cost for the Syrian people. Amnesty International says, "According to the UN around 250,000 people have been killed and 13.5 million people are in urgent need of humanitarian assistance inside Syria. More than 50% of Syria's population is currently displaced. One-in-every-two of those crossing the Mediterranean this year – half a million

people – were Syrians escaping the conflict in their country. More than 4.5 million refugees from Syria are in just five countries Turkey, Lebanon, Jordan, Iraq and Egypt."
<https://www.amnesty.org/en/latest/news/2016/02/syrias-refugee-crisis-in-numbers/>

In a detailed and extensive essay, the Daily Mail reported:

"Iran is shoring up the Syrian regime from a secret HQ in Damascus nicknamed 'the Glasshouse' – and commanding a huge covert army in support of Assad, according to leaked intelligence passed by activists to MailOnline.

"Western analysts have so far placed the total Iranian-led Shia force at just 16,000.

The dissidents make the claim that Iran now commands about 60,000 Shia troops in Syria – 15,000 more men than Britain took into the 2003 Iraq war – while Assad's army has been reduced to just 50,000 soldiers.

"In addition, the Lebanese militant group Hezbollah, which has an independent command structure but operates in close coordination with Iran, has about 10,000 troops in the country, they say.

"The intelligence passed to MailOnline claims that Tehran has spent a staggering $100billion on the conflict since 2011, including hardware and support for Assad's regime.

"Millions of dollars in cash is regularly delivered at the Iranian airstrip before being transferred to the HQ nicknamed 'the Glasshouse', the dissidents claim.

There it is allegedly stored in the basement under the auspices of head of logistics, Brigadier General Seyyed Razi Mousavi, formerly commander of the elite Quds Force in Syria, and is principally used to pay fighters' salaries.

The revelations come after Tehran took the extraordinary step of allowing Russia to use its airbases to launch attacks in Syria, demonstrating its expanding role.

A Foreign Office spokeswoman told MailOnline: 'Iran's role in fostering instability in the Middle East, including ongoing support for proxy groups and the Assad regime, and the activities of the Quds force, remains a source of serious concern.'"

<http://www.dailymail.co.uk/news/article-3718583/Leaked-intelligence-dossier-reveals-location-secret-Iranian-spymasters-HQ-Syria-codenamed-GLASSHOUSE-Iran-fighters-ground-Assad.html>

Despite all this, Tehran has not been able to secure a victory for Assad after 6 years of heavy investments.

In a National Interest article, entitled "Thanks to Russia, Iran Could Lose Control of the Syrian War," and published in October 2015, Mathew McInnis wrote, "Tehran has been losing the Syrian fight since the civil war broke out on 2011. After major setbacks for Syrian government forces in 2012, Iran persuaded a reluctant Lebanese Hezbollah to send in ground forces in early 2013. That helped stabilize Assad's position for a while, but by 2015 the regime was again at risk of losing its most critical positions near the Mediterranean coast and Damascus. Desperate times apparently drove Iran right into Moscow's arms. ... This new campaign has buy-in from both Tehran and Moscow, but it carries potentially significant costs at the strategic level for Tehran. Russia will have more leverage in negotiations to reach a settlement, the terms of which may not benefit Iran. Retaining Assad, or someone just as pliable for Iran, may not be as important for Putin. ... More differences will be hard to escape in the coming months. Moscow, unlike Tehran, does not want to confront Tel Aviv." <http://nationalinterest.org/blog/the-buzz/thanks-russia-iran-could-lose-control-the-syrian-war-14061>

Meanwhile, Iranian casualties continue to mount in Syria;

<https://www.ft.com/content/22380a4e-144c-11e6-9d98-00386a18e39d>

According to some estimates, as published by The Telegraph, "Almost 700 Iranian soldiers and militia fighters have been killed in Syria's civil war, laying bare the scale and cost of Tehran's intervention to preserve Bashar al-Assad's grip on power. ... Their losses on the battlefield are becoming increasingly severe. About 280 Iranians were killed in Syria between the onset of Russia's intervention on Sept 30 last year and May 2, according to a tally compiled by the Levantine Group, a risk consultancy. The Iranian media reported another 400 "martyrs" in Syria between 2013 and mid-2015." <http://www.telegraph.co.uk/news/2016/05/10/almost-700-iranian-troops-killed-in-syria-to-preserve-bashar-al/>

See also:

- "Iran Incurs Painful Losses in Aleppo": http://english.aawsat. com/2016/08/article55356124/iran-incurs-painful-losses-aleppo-u-n-calls-humanitarian-truce

- "Iran's worst week in Syria: Heavy losses, no exit" <https://english.alarabiya.net/en/views/news/middle-east/2016 /05/10/Iran-s-worst-week-in-Syria-Heavy-losses-no-exit.html>

16 On September 21, 2014, Iran-backed Houthi militias seized Yemen's capital, Sanaa. Iran hoped for a quick victory, but has not materialized after 2 years of conflict.

According to Reuters, "A senior Yemeni security official said Iran had steadily supported the Houthis, who have fought the central government since 2004 from their northern stronghold of Saadah. ... Iran, the first official said, saw victory would be swift in Yemen, unlike in Iraq and Syria, and "with not too much expense". A Western source familiar with Yemen also said the Houthis had been getting training and money." < http://www.reuters.com/ article/us-yemen-houthis-iran-insight-idUSKBN0JT17A20141215>

Despite its heavy investments in Yemen, the regime has not been able to reach its goals of securing a Houthi victory. In addition, through its involvement in Yemen, Tehran has become more isolated regionally, especially after a Saudi-led coalition was formed against the Houthi advance. In March 2015, the Saudis announced a coalition with 9 other countries against the pro-Iranian Houthis. <https://english.alarabiya.net/en/News/ middle-east/2015/03/26/GCC-states-to-repel-Houthi-aggression-in-Yemen-statement-.html>

In April, Houthi forces were driven out of the strategic city of Aden. < http://www.aljazeera.com/news/2015/04/yemen-leader-loyalists-drive-houthis-aden-150403132431234.html>

In August 2015, "Yemeni Prime Minister Khaled Bahah flew into the southern port of Aden from exile in Saudi Arabia on Saturday, after pro-government forces ousted Shiite rebels from the city, an airport source said." (AFP) – < http://www.businessinsider. com/afp-yemen-pm-returns-to-aden-from-saudi-exile-airport-source-2015-8>

Therefore, the regime's "swift victory" has not taken place. Instead, it is now involved in another prolonged conflict in the region, further drawing down on its resources.

17 After the Joint Comprehensive Plan of Action (JCPOA) was announced in July 2015, Khamenei finally approved the nuclear deal "with conditions" in October. < http://www.cnn.com/2015/10/21/middleeast/iran-nuclear-deal/>

The nuclear deal was clearly forced on Khamenei. Even as late as August 2016, he "distanced himself from the nuclear agreement reached with major powers a year ago, accusing the United States of failing to honor pledges in the accord and citing "the futility of negotiations with the Americans." <http://www.nytimes.com/2016/08/02/world/middleeast/iran-ayatollah-nuclear.html>

Earlier, in October 2015, he "offered veiled criticism of Iran's nuclear negotiating team, saying that its members had been alert, but that the opposite parties "had found chances" and made "damaging moves against Iran's national interests" in the talks."

He had initially made strict public demands and red lines, most of which were later not adhered to by his own negotiating team. In April 2015, for example, after an interim deal was reached in Lausanne, he had "demanded that all sanctions on Iran be lifted at the same time as any final agreement with world powers on curbing Tehran's nuclear program is concluded." He added, "I neither support nor oppose the deal." <http://www.reuters.com/article/us-iran-nuclear-rouhani-idUSKBN0N00EQ20150409>

Khamenei has always been skeptical and unwilling to abandon the nuclear program. But, it seems that sanctions forced his hands. "Khamenei, who holds the highest office in the Islamic Republic with powers to overrule laws, has taken a skeptical stand on the nuclear talks. But he has also repeatedly endorsed Rouhani's course on ending the economically crippling nuclear stand-off." <http://www.reuters.com/article/us-iran-nuclear-khamenei-idUSKBN0LC08220150208>

The sanctions had a crippling effect on Iran's already mismanaged economy. A 2015 World Bank report "estimated that the tightening of U.S. and European Union sanctions led to a loss of $17.1 billion in export revenue from 2012 to 2014, the equivalent of 4.5 percent of

Iran's gross domestic product. The economy contracted at a rate of 6.8 percent in 2012 and 1.9 percent in 2013 ... Foreign direct investment has also plummeted and is likely to return only slowly. The bank's report said foreign direct investment tumbled from $4 billion in 2010 to "a complete halt in 2012" and still amounts to less than $2 billion. After sanctions were tightened, automobile production fell to 700,000 cars from 1.6 million. Pharmaceutical exports worth $2.5 billion prior to 2012 have tumbled but could resume." <https://www.washingtonpost.com/business/economy/what-ending-sanctions-on-iran-will-mean-for-the-countrys-economy/2015/08/12/2c3a9942-3d17-11e5-b3ac-8a79bc44e5e2_story.html>

If it were not for the heavy cost of the sanctions, in all likelihood, Tehran would have continued its nuclear ambitions as a strategic requirement. In August 2005, "The commander of Iran's Islamic Revolutionary Guards Corps (IRGC) said ... that nuclear capabilities will guarantee the survival of the Islamic Republic. Referring to Tehran's nuclear pursuits, Major General Rahim Safavi told a gathering of members of the paramilitary Bassij in universities, Technology is a vital factor for political regimes in defending themselves. Technological superiority has been and will continue to be the strategic cornerstone for the defence of nations." http://www.iranfocus.com/en/index.php?option=com_content&view=article&id=3286:iran-revolutionary-guards-chief-nuclear-capability-ensures-our-survival&catid=8:nuclear&Itemid=113

In 2007, written evidence provided to the British Parliament's Select Committee on Foreign Affairs stated, "With widespread internal discontent and pressure from the international community over its support for terrorism and nuclear programmes, the regime sees the acquisition of nuclear weapons as the only means to guarantee its survival. To achieve this, the regime has given carte blanche to the IRGC to increase internal repression, while aggressively advancing its nuclear weapons programmes. The regime is well aware that any waning on either of these issues will result in its implosion by bolstering the Iranian people's demand for a change of regime, while at the same time pulling the rug from underneath the feet of the IRGC, who are relying on the acquisition of nuclear weapons. It is for this reason that Ahmadinejad has made clear that the regime will not back down an iota from its nuclear ambitions."

<http://www.publications.parliament.uk/pa/cm200708/cmselect/cmfaff/142/142we03.htm>

In the end, Khamenei was forced to retreat from the regime's strategic and vital nuclear weapons program.

18 On April 14, 2013, Massoud Nili, senior economic advisor in the current government, made some remarkable observations in a TV interview. His remarks were later covered by a state-run daily, which said Nili "went through the number of jobs created in the five and ten year periods from 1956 to 2011. In this setting, the current government has had the lowest job creation record of the past 50 years. If we look at the number of jobs created and the number of people unemployed during the years 2006 to 2011, the number of net new jobs created was around 14,200, which is negligible. ... Net new jobs created during the Holy Defence period (Iran-Iraq war in the 1980s), when the country was involved in a full-fledged 8-year war, was around 200,000 per year – in other words, 14 times the current numbers. This is while in this period, we've had the highest level of oil revenues in Iran's history.

Average annual increase in the number of jobs created in the country (1,000 people)

2006-2011	2001-2006	1996-2001	1991-1996	1986-1991	1976-1986	1966-1976	1956-1966
14.2	695.4	485.4	295	419.1	220.2	194.1	95.1

Looking at this table, we come to a remarkable and, of course, troubling realization. Although between the years 2006 to 2011, the country's annual foreign currency revenues were, on average, two to three times more than previous years, but the number of jobs created between 2006 to 2011 was practically zero! Dr. Nili says that we are witnessing a bizarre and rare economic phenomenon: economic growth without job creation!" (*Asr-e Iran*, April 17, 2013).

19 In 2014, France's largest bank BNP Paribas SA agreed to pay a record $9B in fines for sanctions violations (Bloomberg, June 30, 2014). London-based HSBC was fined $1.9B (Reuters, December 11, 2012). ING Bank of the Netherlands Agreed to forfeit $619 Million for illegal transactions with Iranian entities

(Department of Justice Press Release, June 12, 2012). In 2009, Credit Suisse paid a fine of $536M "to settle accusations by the United States government and New York State authorities that it violated sanctions by helping Iran and other countries secretly funnel hundreds of millions of dollars through American banks" (The New York Times, December 15, 2009). In the same year, Lloyds TSB agreed to pay a fine of $350M to settle charges it altered records for clients from Iran (Department of Justice Press Release, January 9, 2009). In 2010, Barclays agreed to pay $298M in fines (Department of Justice Press Release, August 18, 2010). And, Standard Chartered agreed in 2012 to pay $327M to resolve allegations that it violated U.S. sanctions against Iran (Reuters, December 10, 2012).

20 As The Economist explained in December 2016: "Domestic issues are a further obstacle for employment. The Iranian economy remains dominated by public and semi-public enterprises, which further entrenched their position during the isolation enforced by years of sanctions. The sprawling business empire of the Revolutionary Guards is particularly dominant. By some accounts, the Guards control about a quarter of the economy. Small and medium businesses, the traditional engine of job creation, have struggled to emerge. Running a private company in Iran is fiendishly difficult: the country ranks 120 out of 190 in the World Bank's ease of doing business index. Nor is there much financing to go around. Some 12% of the loans on the books of Iranian banks are non-performing—though the true figure is probably higher. As a result, banks can only lend at steep prices; real interest rates currently stand at about 9%. Moreover, a disproportionate share of the financing goes to the public sector. Iran's job market will face more headwinds, at least in the medium term." See "Why Iran is finding it hard to create jobs," *The Economist*, December 5, 2016. <http://www.economist.com/blogs/economist-explains/2016/12/economist-explains-4>

ABOUT NCRI-US

National Council of Resistance of Iran-US Representative Office acts as the Washington office for Iran's Parliament-in-exile, which is dedicated to the establishment of a democratic, secular, non-nuclear republic in Iran.

NCRI-US, registered as a non-profit tax-exempt organization, has been instrumental in exposing many nuclear sites of Iran, including the sites in Natanz, and Arak, the biological and chemical weapons program of Iran, as well as its ambitious ballistic missile program.

NCRI-US has also exposed the terrorist network of the Iranian regime, including its involvement in the bombing of Khobar Towers in Saudi Arabia, the Jewish Community Center in Argentina, its fueling of sectarian violence in Iraq and Syria, and its malign activities in other parts of the Middle East.

Visit our website at **www.ncrius.org**

You may follow us on   twitter 🐦   @ncrius

Follow us on   f facebook.   NCRIUS

You can also find us on   Instagram   NCRIUS